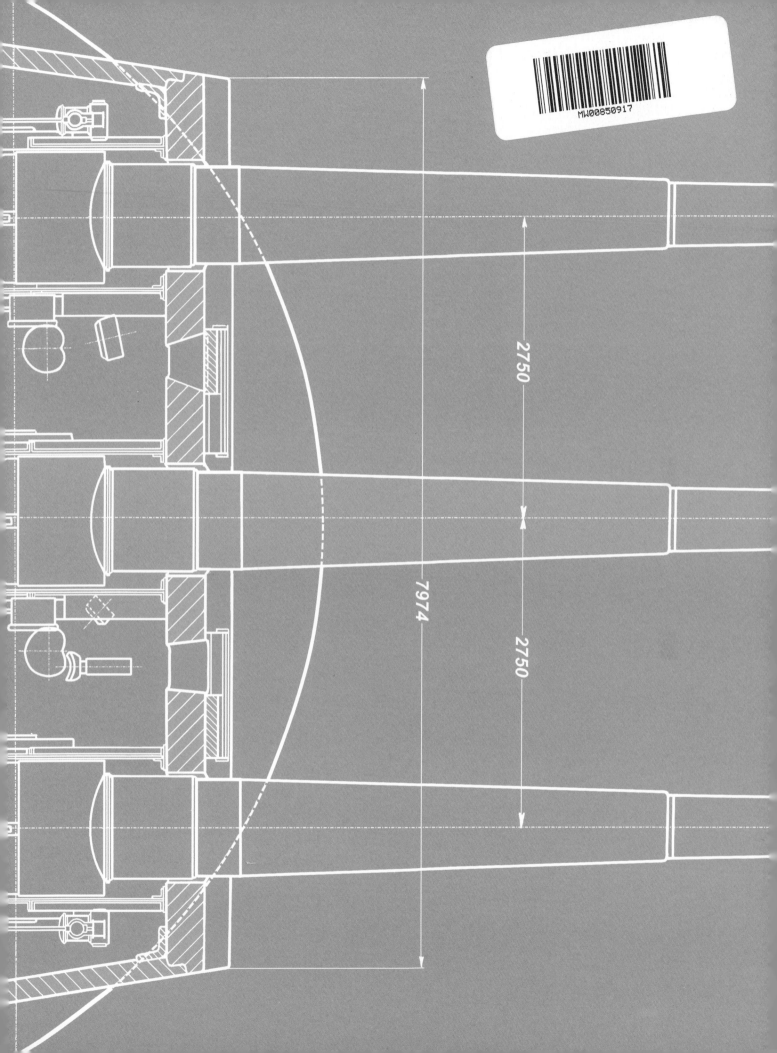

2750

2750

7974

Originally published as *Überschwere Panzerprojekte:
Konzepte und Entwürfe der Wehrmacht* by Motorbuch Verlag,
Stuttgart © 2016 Motorbuch Verlag
Translated from the German by David Johnston

Library of Congress Control Number: 2019935794

Cover design by Justin Watkinson
Type set in Helvetica Neue LT Pro

ISBN: 978-0-7643-5865-4
Printed in China

Published by Schiffer Publishing, Ltd.
4880 Lower Valley Road
Atglen, PA 19310
Phone: (610) 593-1777; Fax: (610) 593-2002
E-mail: Info@schifferbooks.com
Web: www.schifferbooks.com

For our complete selection of fine books on this and related
subjects, please visit our website at www.schifferbooks.com.
You may also write for a free catalog.

Schiffer Publishing's titles are available at special discounts
for bulk purchases for sales promotions or premiums. Special
editions, including personalized covers, corporate imprints, and
excerpts, can be created in large quantities for special needs.
For more information, contact the publisher.

We are always looking for people to write books on new and
related subjects. If you have an idea for a book, please contact
us at proposals@schifferbooks.com.

Contents

Foreword

While working on my book on the *Maus* battle tank (Schiffer Books, 2017), other very interesting German tank projects came into focus. This led to the book on *Wehrmacht* heavy tanks, the focus of which was the further use of the 128 mm L/55 gun.

This third part deals with the superheavy tank designs that came about at the same time. These tanks received their preferential treatment because of Hitler's great interest in heavy armored vehicles. Since other nations were known to be involved in the development of heavy tanks, Hitler wanted to ensure that the German designs maintained a sustained superiority.

This book illuminates the backgrounds behind these developments, describes the technical details of the projects in question, and thus makes it possible to follow the history of many developments. Their designers sought new solutions and broke new ground, with often-unproven technologies. Frequently, however, serious bottlenecks in materials and production capacity hindered these new developments.

Another objective of this book is to counter with facts and figures certain claims and theories about these superheavy armaments projects circulating in the literature. There exist the most fantastic ideas and information, particularly about the 1,000- and 1,500-ton projects, and this begins with the names "Rat" and "Monster," which are pure invention.

I am grateful for the proven help with this book provided by Wolfgang Fleischer of Freital, my daughter Juliane and Barbara Maiwald for their literary support, and Rolf Hilmes for his technical advice; also helpful were Wolfgang Schneider, Joachim Deppmeyer, Yuri Pascholok, Falk Springer, the Mercedes-Benz Classic Archive, the Military Archive Freiburg, the federal Archive of Coblenz, and Bovington Tank Museum for documents and photographs, as well as my daughter Sabine for her patience and care during the work on this book.

Introduction

To be more precise, this book should be called "Adolf Hitler's Superheavy Tank Projects," since as a rule the contracts for the creation of these designs were issued by Hitler over the heads and needs of the *Wehrmacht*, or, to be more precise, the army.

The design bureaus began busying themselves with the development of heavy tanks after the first tank operations of the First World War. As were the German and English militaries, the then Soviet Union military was fascinated by these designs. The idea behind them was to transfer experiences from naval warfare to land warfare. The armored vehicles were supposed to move over land the way that battleships moved on the sea, and to be able to eliminate all resistance from any direction simultaneously and also help break through heavily fortified positions and lines of bunkers. These "land cruisers" were usually armed with a number of guns in several turrets. The first design to become reality after the First World War was the British A1 E1 Independent, which subsequently influenced international tank development and led it into a dead end. Examples of tanks inspired by it include the Soviet T-35 multiturret tank, the German *Neubaufahrzeug*, the American M6 heavy tank, and the French Char 2C breakthrough tank.

The constant increases in armor protection and armament in response to the improved effectiveness of antitank weapons led to ever more absurd designs. Apart from these "land battleships" and mobile bunkers, as well as the *Maus* battle tank, during the Second World War Germany developed additional projects with ever-heavier armor and armament. In the process, the combat weights of these armored vehicles and the associated technical expenditures rose immeasurably. The result was the 1,000-ton project under designer Edward Grote, developed on the basis of the "fortress tank" he had designed in the Soviet Union, while on paper Krupp produced armored heavy howitzers with weights of 1,000 and 1,500 tons. The name of the 1,000-ton, 600 mm heavy howitzer that was pursued was *Urling*, whose moniker involuntarily suggested the uselessness of the project: an *Urling* is a figure from the past who is rooted in the past, and these superheavy concepts were similarly backward looking and outdated and were nothing more than a huge waste of resources.

Michael Fröhlich
Dresden, Germany, summer 2016

CHAPTER 1

From the *Panzerkampfwagen "Löwe"* (Lion) to *"Maus"* (Mouse)

During a meeting with leading Krupp engineers Dorn and Woelfert, *Oberst* Fichtner, head of the Army Ordnance Office's *Wa Prüf* 6 (Development and Testing Department), asked them to consider development of a tank weighing approximately 75 tons and armed with a high-performance gun. Their proposal with information on weight, performance, and the like was to be submitted to *Oberst* Fichtner sometime after mid-October 1941, under conditions of secrecy. The Army Ordnance Office was still feeling the effects of the appearance of the Soviet KV-I and KV-II heavy tanks following the invasion of the USSR, which had come as an unpleasant surprise to the Germans. The representatives of Krupp and *Wa Prüf* 6 met again in Berlin on October 23 to discuss the basic parameters of this heaviest tank. Just a week later, another meeting took place at Krupp in Essen to discuss the turret planned for the VK 7200 project (an erroneous designation). The "general data" for the project, now designated VK 7001 (Experimental 70-Ton Design, Version 1), which was subsequently put down in writing, defined the key points.

The Army Ordnance Office was not yet clear as to the project's armament; however, the *Wa Prüf* 6 requested that the gun be able to move vertically between +20 and −10 degrees and have a traverse range of 360 degrees. On November 11, 1941, *Wa Prüf* 4/VIII suggested that the

VK 7001: Initial Thoughts	
Weight	maximum about 80.5 tons
Power plant	Daimler-Benz MB 507 torpedo boat diesel engine with an output of 800 hp at 2,200 rpm and a more powerful version producing 1,000 hp at 2,400 rpm
Performance	maximum speed of 25 mph or 27 mph
Armor	turret and hull 5.5" of frontal armor, 3.9" on sides
Crew	five men, three in turret

Ballistic Data

Projectile weight was 64.5 lbs. for a 128 mm L/3.9 armor-piercing round and 57 lbs. for a 128 mm L/4.5 high-explosive round. While the armor-piercing shell was to achieve an initial velocity of 2,756 fps, the initial velocity of the howitzer round was 2,936 fps. According to the *Wa Prüf* 6 the propellant charge was to have a standard weight of 27.3 lbs. Further gun specifications are based on a gas pressure of 41,247 psi. The 128 mm barrel's dimensions were a barrel length of 231.5", barrel volume of 4,955 in.³ and a barrel cross section of 20.46 in.². The only difference lay in the cartridge system. Krupp had two different barrels to choose from: a 3.6-ton gun barrel for a cartridge diameter of 6" and a 4.6-ton barrel for a cartridge diameter of 7". The use of identical propellant quantities resulted in different lengths for the shells: the high-explosive variants with the larger diameter were 54.6" long, compared to the shell with the smaller diameter, which was an impressive 65.7" long. Because of the shorter L/3.9 shell used, the armor-piercing cartridge was somewhat smaller.

performance of the gun should enable it to penetrate 180 mm (7 inches) of armor plate with a strength of 80 kg/mm², given a firing range of 3,280 feet (ft.) and an impact angle of 60 degrees. Apparently the industry did not react quickly enough, and during a consultation meeting on November 28, 1941,

Wa Prüf 6 urgently requested proposals for the armament of the VK 7001 tank. Another meeting, this time on December 16, led to a concrete schedule: the first ballistic data for the 128 mm gun became available on January 10, 1942.

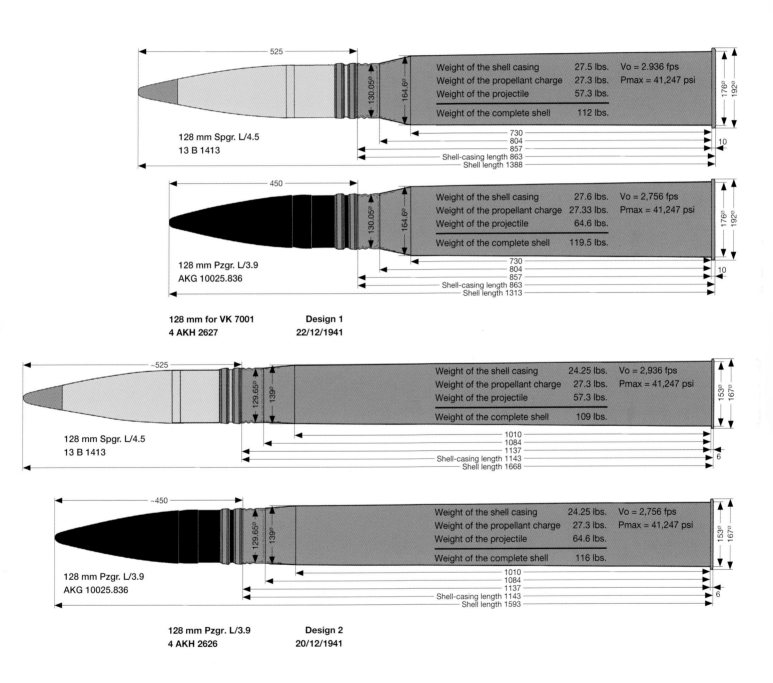

128 mm Spgr. L/4.5
13 B 1413

Weight of the shell casing	27.5 lbs.	Vo = 2.936 fps
Weight of the propellant charge	27.3 lbs.	Pmax = 41,247 psi
Weight of the projectile	57.3 lbs.	
Weight of the complete shell	112 lbs.	

128 mm Pzgr. L/3.9
AKG 10025.836

Weight of the shell casing	27.6 lbs.	Vo = 2,756 fps
Weight of the propellant charge	27.33 lbs.	Pmax = 41,247 psi
Weight of the projectile	64.6 lbs.	
Weight of the complete shell	119.5 lbs.	

128 mm for VK 7001 — **Design 1** — **4 AKH 2627** — **22/12/1941**

128 mm Spgr. L/4.5
13 B 1413

Weight of the shell casing	24.25 lbs.	Vo = 2,936 fps
Weight of the propellant charge	27.3 lbs.	Pmax = 41,247 psi
Weight of the projectile	57.3 lbs.	
Weight of the complete shell	109 lbs.	

128 mm Pzgr. L/3.9
AKG 10025.836

Weight of the shell casing	24.25 lbs.	Vo = 2,756 fps
Weight of the propellant charge	27.3 lbs.	Pmax = 41,247 psi
Weight of the projectile	64.6 lbs.	
Weight of the complete shell	116 lbs.	

128 mm Pzgr. L/3.9 — **Design 2** — **4 AKH 2626** — **20/12/1941**

The First Designs:
The Krupp W 1648 Project

On January 21, 1942, Krupp director Dr. Müller and Engineer Woelfert of Krupp AK met again at a conference held by *Oberst* Fichtner, the head of *Wa Prüf* 6, in Berlin. The participants discussed the development and technical details of the VK 7001 superheavy tank. The first Krupp design—designation W 1648—was an 82-ton vehicle with 4.7 inches of frontal armor and 3.9 inches of side armor. The planned maximum speed was 21.75 miles per hour (mph), and eighty rounds of ammunition were to be carried inside the tank. This design was well received by *Oberst* Fichtner. Because of the desired performance requirements, Dr. Müller proposed a 100 mm L/70 gun, whereupon *Oberst* Müller informed him that Hitler desired a larger caliber. As well, the gun was to be capable of firing armor-piercing sabot ammunition. A loading mechanism was also seen as necessary for the larger-caliber gun's heavy ammunition, even at the cost of a lower firing rate. *Oberst* Fichtner proposed doing away with the machine gun apertures in the bow and rear of the turret and replacing them with Russian-style plugs.

The participants agreed on the turret arrangement: a rear-mounted turret with both the drive and machine systems mounted in front of it would lead to unacceptable conditions for the crew because of the resulting heart and exhaust fumes. As well, this arrangement would result in much undesirable dead space between the driver and the fighting compartment. A central turret arrangement provided stable road-holding characteristics; however, with this arrangement an unavoidably large barrel overhand had to be accepted.

Weight Questions: 79 Tons or 88 Tons?

According to *Wa Prüf* 6, the front drive offered major advantages over rear drive: the vehicle was shorter, and the tracks effectively cleaned themselves of mud and snow, which improved operating reliability. However, the main subject of the meeting was the question of whether a 79-ton or an 88-ton tank was preferable for the VK 7001 project.

Oberst Fichtner favored the heavier type, since it promised a greater advance in the development of armor thickness for the future and a greater distance than the VK 4501 (P) *Tiger*, then under development. All the participants agreed, however, that as an intermediate stage, the 79-ton vehicle could be put into production more quickly. Also, the test phase for testing the rubber-elastic road wheels and the tractability of the relatively long track system could be shortened as a result.

The question of the engine was also significant. *Oberst* Fichtner thought that the Maybach engine, as envisaged for the VK 4501 (H) design, would be suitable for the 79-ton vehicle, even though its greater weight would result in maximum speed being lower than that of the Henschel *Tiger*. In his opinion, however, this was not a disadvantage. The Maybach engine together with the transmission and steering system could be taken from the Henschel design, and Krupp AK was to receive the necessary documentation from *Wa Prüf* 6/III.

Another advantage of the lighter variant was that the fifty depressed-center flatcars envisaged for railway transport of the 57-ton *Tiger* would also be suitable for the 79-ton vehicle, whereas a new flatcar would have to be developed for the 88- to 99-ton tank. As well, the heavier vehicle would require the development of a completely new engine, superimposed steering and transmission systems, and the necessary wider tracks, which would require a significantly longer development period. Without the precise specifications, however, Krupp could not begin producing hulls. Not until Krupp had all the documentation could it provide a delivery date for both vehicle types. Dr. Müller of Krupp then gave the documentation for W 1648 to *Oberst* Fichtner, who assumed that the decision on the VK 7001 superheavy tank would be made at a meeting at *Führer* headquarters one week later.[1]

Krupp Project W 1647

The 90-ton version of the VK 7001, with an aft-located turret and a 105 mm gun with a barrel length of L/70, which was also discussed, was designated W 1647. In addition to the previously mentioned disadvantages of this configuration, the vulnerability of the propulsion system's forward-located grating, which made it necessary to install side air shafts, was another weak point. These air shafts exceeded the railroad profile and had to be removed during rail transport. The lack of space made it impossible to carry spare parts, and the unfavorable aft position of the turret probably led to the tank swaying when being driven.

The VK 7001 was also discussed elsewhere on that January day. There, however, talk was less about the basic design and more about concrete technical questions. The participants were Engineer Woelfert of Krupp and *Regierungsoberbaurat* Ernst Kniepkamp of *Wa Prüf* 6/III-*Forschung* (Research). Again, the W 1648 design, with the center-mounted turret, formed the basis. *Oberbaurat* Kniepkamp knew that Maybach was developing the HL 230, an 800 horsepower (hp) gasoline engine with a weight of 2,755 pounds (lbs.). It was supposed to go into production in January 1943. Kniepkamp was one of the most ardent supporters of the Maybach gasoline engines, on which he had done not insignificant design work. This also explains his skepticism toward the at-least-conceivable use of diesel engines, such as the Mercedes-Benz MB 507, which was already in production for motor torpedo boats. This bias on the part of Kniepkamp was to become even more evident in the years to come. He therefore proposed that construction of the 79-ton tank with the Maybach engine go ahead, while the 89-ton design would be addressed later.

In addition to the engine, the power transmission system was another key element. The choices were a Maybach oil Variorex transmission (later called the "Olvar" transmission), an eight-gear ZF transmission (transmission ratio 1:16), and an as-yet-unnamed Pulsier transmission. These transmissions were to begin testing in mid-1942. *Wa Prüf* 6 planned to initially install an L 600 C superimposed steering system, which would later be replaced by a newly developed, simplified steering system with two stages and four Argus clutches. This new system would also be used in the Henschel *Tiger*. The existing backup steering was to make it possible for the tank to turn on the spot. The future bow shape, with a slope of 45 degrees, had to be taken into consideration because the view from the driver's vision flap was better than with a flatter incline. This also reduced the blind spot in front of the tank. If necessary, the driver's cover plate would have to match the slope.

The *Führer* Conference of January 23 and Its Consequences

At a conference on January 23, 1942, Hitler approved the installation of the proposed systems. However, despite this, the Army Ordnance Office was once again supposed to review the suitability of the Porsche systems from the *Tiger (P)*. Professor Porsche gave assurances that his system would also be suitable for a heavier vehicle, provided the speed requirement was lowered. Hitler was prepared to accept a lower speed, but then he recommended an engine output of 800 hp or 1,000 hp, with supercharging as the best solution, and considered a review of the Porsche system from this point of view as mandatory. On the basis of winter experience, Porsche's air-cooled diesel engine had a great advantage, but the Army Ordnance Office had doubts concerning ventilation of the engine while it was submerged. Porsche was certain, however, that this difficulty could be overcome. However the diesel-electric drive required large quantities of "strategic material" (meaning copper), and this increased material consumption displeased Hitler. Nevertheless, the suitability of Porsche's diesel-electric and diesel-hydraulic drive was to be investigated more closely, while the Army Ordnance Office continued to plead for the Maybach 750 hp gasoline engine or the Daimler-Benz 800 hp diesel engine.

Krupp therefore made the Solomon-like suggestion that the engine compartment be made large enough for all engine variants, so that if the smaller engine was chosen, the extra room could be used to bolster the size of the fighting compartment.

Concerning the running gear, Krupp proposed 33-inch road wheels, but as of yet there was insufficient experience with respect to their durability. The planned smoke discharger system in the rear of the tank could be deleted, since a new discharger for installation in the turret was to be tested in the near future. It was introduced later under the designation *Nahkampfwaffe* (close-range weapon).

A significant feature of any tank is its armament. Hitler preferred a large-caliber gun, in part because of its effectiveness against the target, and also because of its range. And so the Army Ordnance Office was again directed to investigate the suitability of Rheinmetall's 128 mm antiaircraft gun. Hitler ordered that two vehicles with different turrets be built: one with a turret for the 105 mm or 128 mm tank cannon (KwK), and a second with a turret for the 150 mm KwK. The construction of two test vehicles also had the advantage of making it possible to carry out modifications on one vehicle while continuing the planned tests with the second. Regarding ammunition, *Wa Prüf* 6 also planned to undertake development of hollow-charge ammunition for use against tanks.

At the invitation of *Oberst* Fichtner, on January 26, 1942, there was a meeting with Dr. Müller in Berlin. Fichtner informed Müller about the progress of tank development resulting from the meeting with the *Führer*: Hitler had agreed to the development and production of a 77-ton tank, whose armor thickness was to be comparable to that of the VK 4501. It was envisaged that the 105 mm gun would be used, as well as existing propulsion and driving elements. Hitler also went along with the Army Ordnance Office's suggestion of using this vehicle, which under certain conditions could be completed relatively quickly, since a study object for an even more heavily armored tank to test new drive elements was under development.

At the end of January 1942, Krupp decided to prepare a vehicle on which both the turret with the 105 mm L/70 tank gun and one with a 150 mm L/40 tank gun could be mounted. A maximum elevation of 35 to 40 degrees was to be possible, so that this large-caliber weapon could also be used purely in the artillery role. Fichtner, however, requested that the use of a gun with a caliber of 128 mm and a barrel length of L/50 be incorporated into the planning, in addition to the 128 mm L/61 antiaircraft gun proposed by Hitler. Depending on time frames, Krupp could cast, press, or weld the armored turret.

This conversation between Fichtner and Müller resulted in the following planning status: Krupp was to build two identical vehicles, plus a turret for the 105 mm gun and another one for the 150 mm gun. On that basis the company created separate schedules for the completion of vehicles and turrets.

In order to adhere to these deadlines, the design-related problems that existed among the Army Ordnance Office, the subcontractors, and the factories had to be completely resolved by the end of February, and the raw materials ordered as soon as possible.

State of Planning at the End of January 1942

Vehicle Schedule:

May 1, 1942:	assignment of sheet metal
August 1, 1942:	essential working diagrams
November 1, 1942:	hull for assembly
April 1, 1943:	completion of first vehicle

Turret Schedule:

August 1, 1942:	essential parts
February 1, 1943:	completion of first turret

The strict timetable demanded many additional meetings and coordination sessions, since the actual work was only now beginning. There were countless details to work out. During a meeting on the program for further development of tank turrets on February 2, 1942, under point 3 Dr. Müller stressed the necessity of determining the smallest possible servicing diameter of a 105 mm L/70 turret so that this could also be mounted on the VK 4501 (P) tank. If necessary, he was prepared to accept a reduction in the gun's elevation range. Delivery of ammunition was to follow the pattern of the 88 mm L/71 tank gun. Alternately, in addition to the 105 mm L/70 turret of the VK 7201 (the VK 7001 was often wrongly thus designated), point 4 envisaged investigating the smallest possible servicing diameter for a tank equipped with a 128 mm L/50 turret or a 150 mm L/40 turret.

Point 5 addressed the examination of the VK 7001 in terms of its suitability for the installation of a second, smaller turret mounting a 75 mm gun. Since there was not sufficient space for this, it was to be determined if a smaller gun with a caliber of 50 to 75 mm could be accommodated on the vehicle for firing high-explosive ammunition for large- and small-quadrant elevations. The Army Ordnance Office had already gained experience with this principle of coaxially coupled tank guns with the *Neubaufahrzeug* tank. This vehicle had a 37 mm L/48 tank gun mounted over a 75 mm L/23.5 tank gun. Such a design was intended to allow tanks and positions to be engaged separately, conserving ammunition for the main gun.

After reviewing the German National Railway's loading profile, Krupp determined that the 105 mm turret fit easily, but that the 150 mm turret exceeded the loading profile in two respects. Reducing the size of the turret seemed impossible, however, and the Army Ordnance Office considered this exceedance acceptable for normal travel, since there had often been such exceedances by the frontline units in the past. For a loaded weight of 99 tons, Krupp took as its starting point a loading platform over rail level height of 1,250 mm (49.2 in.) in empty condition and 1,160 mm (45.7 in.) in loaded condition.

Turret Design

Turret weight with the *Tiger* systems, including interior fittings, was 21 tons, to which was added 2.2 tons of ammunition. Ammunition capacity at that time was seventy-six rounds, of which forty-six rounds were stowed in the turret. The turret of the Porsche *Tiger*, in contrast, weighed 10.6 tons, while the up-armored version weighed 13.8 tons. In the first designs for the VK 7001 tank, the turret weight had been 14 and 18 tons. The later demand for an increased armor thickness from 3.9 to 4.7 inches caused the turret weight to rise to 23.6 tons, however. The servicing diameter with the 105 mm tank gun was 95.25 inches. This dimension caused Kugelfischer Georg Schäfer & Co., which was responsible for making the pivot bearing, serious problems.

The specified bearing bore of 98 inches equated to an external measurement of 108 inches, yet the bearing load required a bearing with tempered groove and an outer diameter of at least 110 inches. Should Krupp insist on the smaller outer diameter of 108 inches, according to Kugelfischer there would be considerable problems in manufacturing the bearings, which would mean delays in delivery and price increases. After a lively exchange of correspondence, on April 24, 1942, the two companies agreed on a pivot bearing size of 98.6 × 108.5 × 3.9 inches. By comparison: the *Tiger (P)* with its 88 mm gun required a servicing diameter of 72.8 inches. *Wa Prüf* 6 still had to decide between an electrically or hydraulically operated traverse drive.

On February 23, 1942, there was another meeting at Krupp, the subject of which was the turret of the VK 7001. Those responsible had originally planned a 93-ton VK 7001 tank with 4.7 inches of frontal armor and 3.9 inches of side armor, using newly developed systems. The military situation, however, quickly forced a change to the construction of two prototype vehicles, which were to be put into production without trials. *Wa Prüf* 6 therefore decided to build a 79-ton tank with the same armor thicknesses as the *Tiger* (3.9 inches frontal, 3 inches side), as well as with its proven systems. The fifty special flatcars then under construction for the 57-ton *Tiger* also favored the lighter version. Two possibilities were once again discussed:

1. **Rear-mounted turret, engine compartment forward:** Krupp feared a more difficult and time-consuming design process. If this configuration proved unsuccessful, a subsequent exchange of turret and engine compartment would be possible only at the risk of threatening production startup.
2. **Turret in the center, engine compartment aft:** Favored by *Wa Prüf* 6, since this configuration had proved itself in all new tank designs. The office was prepared to accept the nose-heaviness caused by the large barrel overhang.

The official replacement of the tank designation VK 7001 with the suggestive designation *Panzerkampfwagen Löwe* took place in March 1942. As previously described, when development of this tank project began, the designation VK 7201 occasionally appeared in the files. Some staff probably decided on the designation VK 7201 on the basis of the vehicle's weight (72 tons); however, this never appeared officially. The same is true of the designation *Panzerkampfwagen* VII, which likewise appears in some documents.

Profile of Requirements for new Tanks, March 1942

On March 5, 1942, the *Wa Prüf 6* of the Army Ordnance Office laid down requirements for a VK 7201 (added in pencil: *PzKpfw. VII "Löwe"*)

- **Combat weight:** 79 tons
- **Speed:** 19 to 22 mph
- **Range:** 5 hours at full power
- **Turret armor:** Front: 3.9" sides: 3.15" rear: 3.9"
- **Hull armor:** Bow: 3.9" sides: 3.14" rear: 3.9" roof: 1.6" floor: 1.2"
- **Armament:** 128 mm or 150 mm gun (was crossed out); instead, a 100 mm KwK L/70, or a 150 mm KwK L/35, 2 to 3 machine guns
- **Crew:** 6
- **Dimensions:** Width: 138" in keeping with railroad loading profile
- **Fording ability:** UK ~315"
- **Ammunition:** ~80 rounds for the gun, 4,000 rounds for the machine guns
- **Radio equipment:** Fu 5 and Fu 2
- **Direction device:** Directional gyro

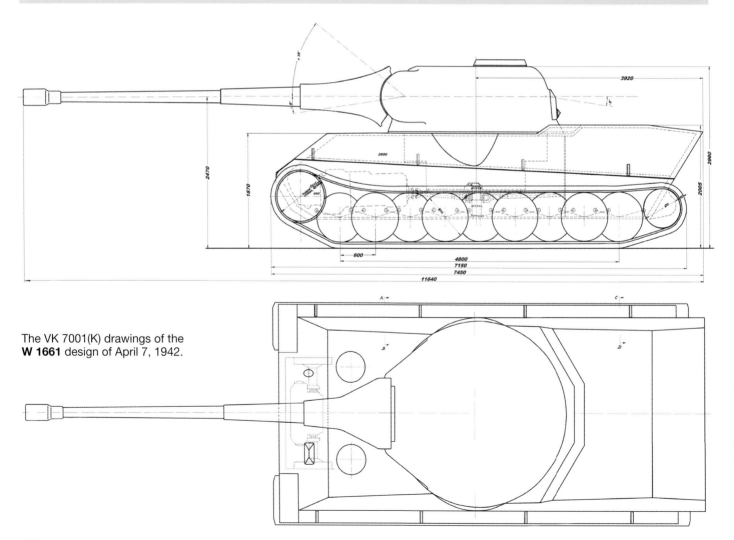

The VK 7001(K) drawings of the **W 1661** design of April 7, 1942.

New Direction:
A 100-Ton (110-Metric-Ton) *Löwe* (Lion)

At the same time, at another armaments conference on March 5, 1942, Hitler issued the "order to the Krupp company that a 100-ton tank, not a 72-ton one, is to be developed as a test vehicle as quickly as possible, with the first test vehicles to be put into operation quickly, in any case prior to the spring of 1943."[2]

Two weeks later, on March 21, 1942, Porsche also received a contract for the independent design of a 100-ton (110-metric-ton) tank. The simultaneous issuing of development contracts to competing firms was supposed to result in an increase in development performance. In the early days of German tank development, as many as four companies had been issued identical development contracts. This practice had to be abandoned, however, as the German armaments production situation deteriorated.

Once again, two experimental vehicles were to be built and tested. One vehicle was to be equipped with a turret while the second would have an equivalent weight of ballast. In design and appearance, the hull was similar to that of the VK 4503 (*Tiger* III, later designated *Tiger* II) then under development. It was envisaged that it would be powered by the twelve-cylinder Maybach HL 210 engine installed in the *Tiger*.

The main armament was to consist of the 105 mm KwK L/70 or, optionally, a 150 mm KwK L/35. The advantages and disadvantages of each caliber (in which the 128 mm KwK was also included) were weighed and considered a number of times. While a smaller caliber had advantages in rate of fire and the amount of ammunition that could be carried, the larger caliber promised greater penetrative ability, better explosive effect, and longer range.

The decision on thicker steel plates was made in April 1942, and the VK 7001 (K) project was now to have 4.7 inches of armor on the front of the hull and turret, 3.9 inches on the upper sides, and 3.1 inches on the lower sides. As a result, the planned weight rose to 99 tons, which in turn led to the W 1658 and W 1661 variants.

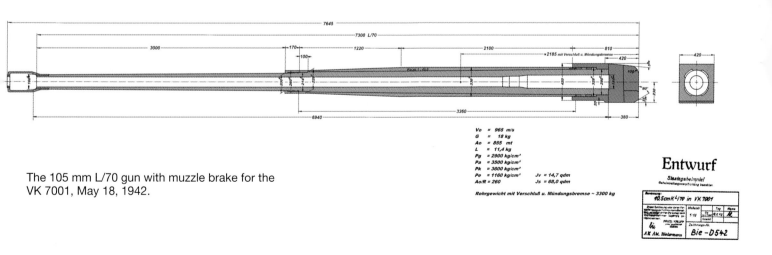

The 105 mm L/70 gun with muzzle brake for the VK 7001, May 18, 1942.

W 1658 Design

This was an 83-ton tank with 3.9 inches of frontal armor and 3.1 inches of side armor. Hull length was 278 inches and track contact surface was 170 inches. The 39-inch-wide track gave a specific ground pressure of 13 lbs. per square inch (psi). With a sink depth of 7.9 inches, the ground pressure value was 10 psi. Optionally, Krupp compared the version with two 330 hp Porsche engines; however, this increased the hull length by 16 inches to 294 inches. Power-to-weight ratio also fell from the approximately 10 hp/ton with one 800 hp Maybach gasoline engine to 8 hp/ton with the Porsche unit.

W 1661 Design

This alternative was a 99-ton tank with 4.7 inches of frontal armor and 3.9 inches of side armor. Hull length was 293 inches, with a track contact surface of 189 inches. With the 39-inch-wide track, specific ground pressure was 13.4 psi; with a sink depth of 7.9 inches, the value was 10.7 psi. To make up for the increased weight, *Wa Prüf* 6 planned to use a 1,000 hp Maybach gasoline engine, which was yet to be designed, and strengthened *Tiger* systems. The use of two Porsche 430 hp diesel engines required that the hull be lengthened by 9.4 inches to 303 inches, and the track contact surface increased to 198 inches. With the same track width, this resulted in a ground pressure of 12.7 psi, which with a sink depth of 7.9 inches was equivalent to 10.25 psi. Power-to-weight ratio followed a similar pattern. The longer hull required with the Porsche engines made it necessary to add another road wheel; however, the Krupp designers saw as an advantage the Porsche engine's lower overall height, which reduced hull and firing height by 2 inches.

Armament and Ammunition

The Army Ordnance Office regarded the 105 mm L/70 gun as insufficiently powerful. To ensure the tank's long-term superiority, Krupp proposed a new turret with more-powerful armament; namely, a 128 mm L/35 gun with a muzzle velocity of 24 feet per second (fps) or a 150 mm L/30 gun with a muzzle velocity of 21 fps. Range suffered as a result, however, which in turn required the use of longer gun barrels. The result was the 128 mm tank gun with 50-caliber lengths and a muzzle velocity of 32 fps, and the 150 mm gun with 40-caliber lengths and a muzzle velocity of 33 fps. Instead of using a separate charge, the gun was to fire fixed ammunition, in order to achieve a rate of fire of four to five rounds per minute. The cartridge used by the 150 mm *Flugabwehrkanone* 50 (antiaircraft gun), which was designated *Gerät* 50 (Device 50), was to serve as the basis, although *Wa Prüf* 6 wanted to reduce projectile weight from 95 to 75 lbs. The already-developed 150 mm *Granatpatrone* weighed a considerable 126 lbs. and was 63 inches long. Despite the clear advantages of lighter ammunition, three more 95-lb. armor-piercing rounds were developed for the *Löwe*: L/3.7, L/3.8, and L/3.9. A 128 mm L/4.5 shell weighing 92 lbs. served as a high-explosive round. The total weight of the 5 ft. long shell was 152 lbs.

Part of this ammunition had to be carried in the rear of the turret in a sort of rucksack. With a shell length of 63 inches, loading the gun was to be possible directly from the "rucksack" in the range of −8 to +10 degrees or even with the barrel elevated 15 degrees. The total aiming area was to be 360 degrees in azimuth and 40 degrees in elevation.

Interestingly, Krupp also offered this turret to Porsche for its VK 100.01 until May 15, 1942. The reason behind this was the *Mäuschen* superheavy tank project,[3] development of which had begun in the meantime.

The decision as to the VK 7001's main armament had still not been made on April 29, 1942, but it was to follow by mid-May. Despite this, Krupp was already planning the production of ten prototypes.

State of Planning, End of April 1942

The following must be ordered:

■ the armor and the major parts by September 1, 1942,

■ the essential parts by October 1, 1942,

■ the remaining parts by November 1, 1942.

In keeping with vehicle deadlines, Krupp requires:

■ the first two turrets by March 1, 1943,

■ three more turrets by April 1, 1943,

the next five turrets by June 1, 1943.

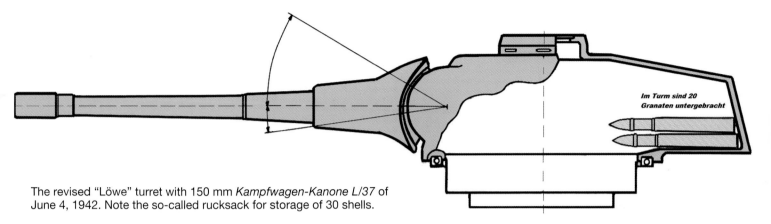

The revised "Löwe" turret with 150 mm *Kampfwagen-Kanone L/37* of June 4, 1942. Note the so-called rucksack for storage of 30 shells.

Im Turm sind 20 Granaten untergebracht

Ten turrets were to be produced monthly, five for the Krupp vehicles and five for the Porsche vehicles. The turret design drawings were to be issued to the departments by mid-May. The guns with muzzle brakes and recuperators had to be readied two months before completion of the turrets.

Two development vehicles were supposed to be delivered first: one vehicle with a turret, and one without a turret but with ballast weight. Since the 1,000 hp Maybach gasoline engine was not yet available, on May 11, 1942, *Wa Prüf* 6 made plans for the 99-ton VK 7001 *Löwe* with a 150 mm KwK L/40 to be powered by two Porsche diesel engines with supercharging, producing a total of 840 hp. A Henschel KLL 800/320 cross-drive steering transmission was to be used, as was either a 12 EV 170 electromagnetic twelve-speed transmission or the Maybach OG 401216 Olvar transmission. Initially, however, the 750 hp Maybach gasoline engine was the only power plant available.

During a conference in Berlin on May 7, 1942, Dr. Roland, chairman of the Central Committee Tanks and Prime Movers, informed all the participants in writing about Program III for the period January 1 to December 31, 1943. Among other things, it revealed that the 110-ton *Löwe* tank would not be produced by Krupp. Nevertheless, at a meeting on May 13, 1942, the *Wa Prüf* 6/III asked Krupp for an offer for the engineering design of the VK 7001 tank and the building of two development vehicles, one with a turret and one without a turret but with ballast weight.

The department would make available two engines, two transmissions, one steering transmission, and two sets of tracks. This clearly demonstrated *Wa Prüf* 6's interest in continuing development of the VK 7001 heavy tank, if necessary on its own.

Also on May 13, 1942, Hitler demanded more-rapid progress on the heaviest tank, which was then in the design stage. In his opinion, reducing the vehicle's weight to 77 tons was a mistake; instead he thought that its weight could rise from 110 to 132 tons and that armor protection and a high-performance gun with a caliber length of L/60 to L/72 were more important, in order to achieve a development lead over the expected Russian superheavy tanks. He did not know, however, that Joseph Stalin had canceled production of the roughly 110-ton KV-5 tank from the Kirov works in Leningrad because of the war situation.

The 105 mm L/70 Gun

On May 18, 1942, five days after the meeting mentioned above, *Oberbaurat* Kniepkamp, head of *Wa Prüf* 6/III, canceled the contract for the construction of the two *Löwe* experimental vehicles; on May 26, Krupp issued an internal memo informing all participants of the decision, and halted design work on the 105 mm L/70 gun. The design documents relating to the VK 7001 turret were to be turned over to Porsche.

The *Wa Prüf* 4/III, however, showed interest in the 105 mm gun, and on May 27, 1943, it issued Krupp a so-called war contract for the "Creation of design and working drawings of a 105 mm L/70 gun with associated targeting and laying devices." The requested 3 × 8-degree antitank gun telescopic sight and the ground stakes from the 88 mm antiaircraft gun made it obvious that it was to be an antitank gun. These stakes were necessary to better anchor the gun for direct fire.

According to *Wa Prüf* 1/VII, the shape of the shell case was to be similar to that of the 128 mm antiaircraft gun, and after a slight change in length it was to be retracted with a newly prepared retraction matrix. One hundred shell casings were to suffice for the initial experiments. The ballistic data

that *Wa Prüf* 1/VII requested from Krupp revealed the following information for the 105 mm L/70 gun:

■ Muzzle velocity (V_0) = 3,166 fps or 3,527 fps
■ Projectile weight = 40 lbs. or 34 lbs.
■ Charge (propellant) weight = 25 lbs.
■ Barrel weight = 7,275 lbs. with breech and muzzle brake
■ Utilization pressure = 41,248 psi
■ Design pressure = 51,204 psi

The cost of a 105 mm barrel, which was to be mounted on a 210 mm *Mörser* 18, was 16,000 *Reichsmarks*. *Wa Prüf* 4 wanted to use the 105 mm gun already in production as s test weapon for the 105 mm high-performance antitank gun then being planned. For this purpose, Krupp was to extend the barrel length to 284 inches. With a shell weighing 34.4 lbs., the planned conical barrel achieved a theoretical muzzle velocity of 3,527 fps. *Wa Prüf* 4/III specified June 1943 as the completion date for this gun. According to Krupp, May 1943 was possible if the gun barrel could be produced with cylindrical sections instead of conical ones. Nothing came of this, since by the end of 1942, the department had lost interest in the 105 mm L/70 barrel, and in January 1943 it was released and *Wa Prüf* 4 used it as a test barrel.

After the leadership had clearly come out in favor of an even-heavier tank, on June 7, 1942, the official decision was made to abandon the *Löwe* project with the 105 mm L/70 gun and instead pursue the *Maus* project with two guns—the 150 mm L/37 and the 75 mm L/24. This ultimately meant the end of the VK 7001 project, but nevertheless, during a meeting with *Oberst* Fichtner on June 19, 1942, Jäger, the advisor for heavy tanks in the armaments ministry, advised Dr. Müller not to completely write off the *Löwe*. Depending on the success of the Porsche *Tiger*, it seemed entirely conceivable that interest in the optional construction of a tank with purely mechanical drive might revive, especially because the first Porsche vehicles were still encountering various problems.

W 1670 Design

And so, all the participants decided to continue optimizing the project. For tactical reasons, Krupp had given the weight of the W 1664 project as 99 tons, while purely theoretically this was only 92.6 tons. There was thus room to maneuver, which led to the W 1670 design with an actual weight of 99 tons. It envisaged a 0.8-inch increase in armor thickness on the front and the sides, to 5.5 inches and 4.7/3.9 inches, respectively.

The view of those responsible at Krupp at that time was clear: "As far as the construction of tanks over 66 tons [such as the *Tiger* with up-armored turret] is even profitable, one should keep the vehicle weight as low as possible in order to combine an adequate weapon and armor with good maneuverability and maximum speed. It should be kept in mind that only an engine system of 800 hp is available. Further, greater armor thickness is of limited value because of the lack of protection for the running gear and complicates the installation of the driver's visor. In most cases 3.9 to 4.7 inches of frontal armor sloped at less than 35 degrees is sufficient, being equal to about 6.3 to 7.9 inches in a vertical surface."[4]

The discussions continued. Because (as mentioned above) the engine question could not be solved satisfactorily, instead of the 99-ton tank with the 150 mm L/37 gun, *Oberst* Fichtner suggested a tank with an edged turret mounting an 88 mm gun and very heavy overall armor, as per drawing W 1668. There was also a proposal to design a particularly flat-pressed turret made of armor plate mounting the 88 mm L/71 gun. Despite the heavy armor, 5.5 inches forward and 5.5/4.7 inches on the sides, by shortening the vehicle it would be possible to achieve a weight of 87 tons, which increased the power-to-weight ratio from 8.9 to 10 hp per ton and maximum speed from 18.5 to 21.75 mph. As well, firing height was lowered from 96.5 to 89 inches. With 88 mm ammunition weighing 50.7 lbs. instead of 150 mm shells weighing 128 lbs., the possible rate of fire was also higher.

Compared to the 66-ton Porsche or Henschel *Tiger*, which were to be armed with the same 88 mm gun, because of the shape of its turret the more heavily armored 88-ton vehicle had fewer shot traps and would have been easier to produce. On a design version without the use of transport tracks, the planned width of 137.8 inches (instead of 128 inches with two-way traffic) still permitted the vehicle to be transported by rail without two-way traffic. But despite all these hypotheses, the VK 7001 project was found to be too light.

Designation	Weight	Armament	Frontal	Side	hp/ton	Vmax
W 1668	80 t	88 mm L/71	5.5"	5.5/4.7"	10	21.75 mph
W 1669	80 t	150 mm L/37	5.5"	3.9/3.15"	10	21.75 mph
W 1670	90 t	150 mm L/37	5.5"	4.7/3.9"	8.9	17–20.5 mph

Krupp AK list for the "Löwe" project from June 19, 1942

	November 1, 1942	February 27, 1942	April 9, 1942
Weight	79 tons	82 tons	84 tons and 99 tons
Engine	Mercedes DB 507 torpedo boat engine 800 hp / 2,200 rpm 1,000 hp / 2,400 rpm diesel		Maybach HL 230 700 hp / 3,000 rpm 800 hp
Transmission	Electromagnetic transmission 12 EV 170 12 gears (later 7 gears)		
Steering	L 600 c superimposition gearbox with three stages (later two stages)		
Suspension	Torsion bar suspension with interleaved rubber-sprung road wheels		
Armor Hull front	5.5"	3.9"	3.9" and 4.7"
Armor Hull sides	3.9"	3.15"	3.15" and 3.9"
Armor Turret front	5.5"		3.9" and 4.7"
Armor Turret sides	3.9"		3.9" and 4.7"
Armor Roof		1.6"	1.6"
Armor Floor		1.2"	
Max. speed	25 mph at 800 hp 27 mph at 1,000 hp		17 mph and 14.3 mph
Crew hull			2 men
Crew turret			3 men
Gun	105, 128 or 150 mm	105 mm L/70	105 mm L/70
Elevation/traverse	+20° / −10° 360°		+38° / −8° 360°
Operating circle diameter		94.25"	
Turret weight		21 tons	
Number of rounds		76 shells 46 in turret	
Track length		147'	
Track width		29.5"	31.5"
Track weight		ca. 250 kg/m	
Track contact length		170"	170" and 189"
At sink depth of 20 cm			
Spec. ground pressure			1.10 and 1.17 kg/cm²
At sink depth of 20 cm			
Overall length with gun			442" and 458"
Overall length without gun		279"	277" and 293"
Overall width			143"
Track gauge			111"
Ground clearance			19"
Overall height with cupola			
Overall height without cupola			116"
Firing height			97"

Overview of the many developed variants of the VK 7001 project

April 23, 1942	April 23, 1942	May 1, 1942	May 11, 1942	May 11, 1942
88 tons	90 tons	90 tons	75 tons	90 tons
Maybach HL 230 750–800 hp gasoline	Maybach HL 230 750/800 hp gasoline or 2 × Porsche without supercharger 660 hp gasoline or 2 × Porsche with supercharger 840 hp diesel or more powerful Maybach 1,000 hp gasoline		Maybach HL 230 700 hp / 3,000 rpm gasoline 840 hp diesel	2 × Porsche with supercharger 840 hp diesel
				see April or Olvar OG 401216
				KLL 800/320 superimposition gearbox
3.9"	4.7"	4.7"	3.9"	4.7"
3.15"	3.9"	3.15/3.9"	3.15"	3.15/3.9"
3.9"	4.7"	4.7"	3.9"	4.7"
3.9"	4.7"	4.7"	3.9"	4.7"
1.6"	1.6"	1.6"	1.6"	1.6"
with new steering transmission 21.7 mph			18.6 mph	18.6 mph
105 mm L/70	105 mm L/70	105 mm L/70	105 mm L/70	150 mm L/40
				+30° / –7° 360°
80 shells	80 shells	80 105 mm shells		50 150 mm shells 30 in turret
35.4"	39.37"	35.4" or 39.37"	29.5"	35.4" or 39.37"
170"	195.25"	195.25"	170.8"	195.25"
224"	246.5"	246.5"		246.5"
1.0 kg/cm^2	12.8 lbs./in.^{2}	14.2 or 12.8 lbs./in.^{2}	15.9 lbs./in.^{2}	14.2 or 12.8 lbs./in.^{2}
0.78 kg/cm^2	10.2 lbs./in.^{2}	11.4 or 10.2 lbs./in.^{2}		11.4 or 10.2 lbs./in.^{2}
441"	459"	459"	443"	423"
275"	293"	293"	274"	304.7"
150.8"	159"	150.8" or 159"	139"	150.8" or 159"
115"	119"	115" or 119"	109.8"	115" or 119"
19.7"	19.7"	19.7"	19.7"	19.7"
121.5"	121"	121"		120"
117.5"	117"	117"	115"	
98"	98"	98"	98.8"	97.6"

From *Löwe* to *Mäuschen*

Krupp received a contract from the Army Ordnance Office to design a turret for the *Mäuschen* by July 17, 1942. The turret had a 150 mm L/37 gun and a 75 mm KwK 37 with a length of L/24. *Wa Prüf* 6 specified armor thicknesses of 9.8 inches forward, 7.8 inches on the sides, and 3.15 inches on the roof. The weight of the turret was not supposed to exceed 63 tons, its range of traverse was to be 360 degrees, and

the elevation range of the two guns was to be –7 to +25 degrees. The 25-ton turret of the *Löwe* tank could not meet this requirements profile, especially since it did not seem possible to Krupp to produce the rounded armor plates projected by the *Löwe* project.

On June 23, 1942, Professor Porsche presented his first designs. Hitler accepted the designs in principle, but he demanded thicker armor and heavier armament—the 150 mm L/37 or 105 mm L/70 gun. Hitler preferred the latter because

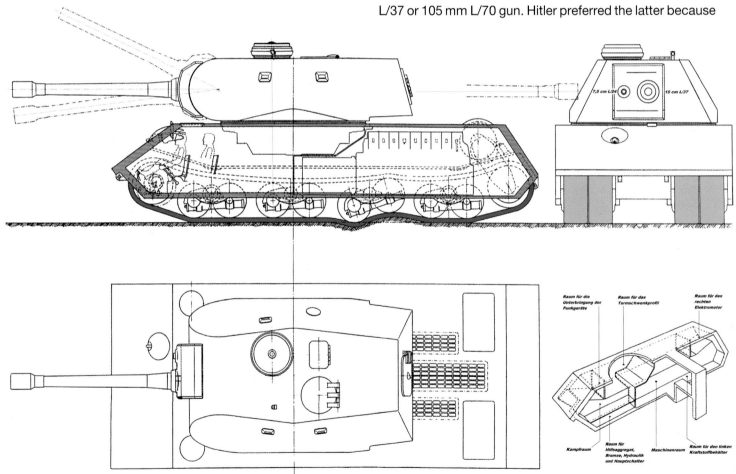

The reinforced Krupp turret with 150 mm and 75 mm guns envisaged for both *Maus* tanks, here in a drawing for the "Porsche *Maus*" dated October 25, 1942

of its higher rate of fire and large ammunition capacity. The turret was to be capable of accommodating either gun. On August 21, 1942, Krupp ordered a 1:10 scale wooden model for a welded turret of rolled plates with a 150 mm and a 75 mm gun. This turret design was repeated in Porsche's Maus design of October 25, 1942.

During a meeting at the end of November 1942, Krupp reported on the search for a suitable engine for its own *Maus* design. The first choices were two Daimler-Benz liquid-cooled gasoline engines, the MB 501 producing 1,200–1,500 hp and the MB 503 producing 1,200 hp. If delivery was not possible because of schedule difficulties, Krupp intended to use the Maybach HL 230 gasoline engine from the *Tiger* tank, producing 700 hp at 3,000 revolutions per minute (rpm), or the MB 507 diesel engine, used to power S-boats, which delivered 800–1,000 hp at 2,200–2,400 rpm. For his *Maus*, Porsche favored the Daimler-Benz DB 603 aero-engine, which produced 1,375 hp at 2,300 rpm. The short list of transmissions for the Krupp *Maus* included a reinforced Olvar transmission for 1,200 hp from Maybach, the ZF constant-mesh transmission, or else the electromagnetic transmission, also from the Zahnradfabrik Friedrichshafen (ZF).

There were no steering systems for these high-performance power plants, however. Two transmissions first had to be built for testing. The key data for both included a steering ratio of 1:2, a shift speed of 1:16, and a maximum speed of 18 mph. This was based on a vehicle weight of 187 tons and an engine output of 1,200 hp. Krupp and *Wa Prüf* 6 envisaged a deadline of September 1, 1943. Accommodation of a 1,200 hp engine and the associated cooling system caused difficulties. *Wa Prüf* 6 specified that the engine should be mounted in the rear of the hull. Should the engines and transmission not be available at that time, the design was to be adapted to 700 to 800 hp, which would reduce maximum speed to just 12.5 mph.[5]

Interestingly, this combination of components was also supposed to be used in the planned R-1 tracked vehicle, mounting a 380 mm C/34 L/48.5 naval gun, and the R-2, with a 280 mm C/34 naval gun with a length of L/54.5, both of which were envisaged for the coastal defense role.

The Krupp *Maus* and the Porsche *Maus*: A Comparison

On December 1, 1942, during an armaments conference, Professor Porsche and Dr. Müller reported on the status of their respective designs. Hitler expected the first experimental vehicles from both companies by the summer of 1943; construction was to take place at Krupp. Hitler demanded a monthly production of five *Mäuschen*, but since the decision had not yet been made on which gun to use, he hoped for a presentation on the penetrative abilities of the planned alternatives: the 150 mm L/38 tank gun, the 127 mm naval cannon, the 128 mm *Flugabwehrkanone* 40 (antiaircraft gun), and the 128 mm gun with longer caliber length.[6]

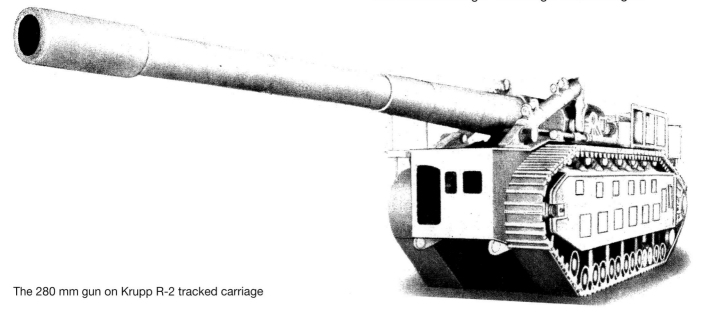

The 280 mm gun on Krupp R-2 tracked carriage

On December 8, 1942, there was another meeting between Krupp's artillery design department and the Army Ordnance Office's *Wa Prüf* 6. Krupp proposed a 143-ton tank, based on propulsion elements of the Henschel *Tiger* III (later *Tiger* II) with a centrally mounted turret. Elements in favor of this solution included its better steering ratio of 1:1.43 (instead of the roughly 1:2.5 of the Porsche version) and its better ground pressure of 1.1 kg/cm² (with sink depth), compared to the Porsche design's 18 psi. Also, the Krupp design was 44 tons lighter than the 187-ton Porsche, which also promised lower fuel consumption and savings in raw materials and working hours. In addition, according to Krupp, rail transport would be possible without stopping two-way traffic; however, this assessment was based on the use of transport tracks and the associated elimination of running-gear armor, which weighed against the Krupp design.

Another disadvantage resulted from the 700 hp Maybach gasoline engine, which, with a power-to-weight ratio of just 5.4 hp per ton, was too weak. However, *Oberbaurat* Kniepkamp of *Wa Prüf* 6 promised a 1,000 hp engine with a power-to-weight ratio of 7.5 hp per ton by September 1943. (Ernst Kniepkamp was probably referring to the Maybach HL 232 gasoline engine with mechanical fuel injection and mechanical supercharging; however, Maybach was unable to make the engine production-ready before the war ended.)

Krupp nevertheless designed the reduction gearing and steering transmission for this high-performance figure. Kniepkamp also demanded a lighter turret, which at the time represented 35 percent of the total vehicle weight. In comparison, the *Tiger*'s turret accounted for just 17 to 20 percent. Its position in the center of the hull provided a better slope angle, even better than that of the *Tiger* I and *Tiger* III. Arguing against the aft arrangement, as used by the Porsche version, was the vehicle's center of gravity, which was 15.75 inches farther to the rear. Thus the Krupp version's UK system (underwater driving system) could not be completely adopted

The fourteen-axle depressed-center flatcar made by Simmering-Graz-Pauker AG.
Deppmeyer Collection

20 703

from the *Tiger* as planned. As well, the available engine space—as in the *Panther* or *Tiger*—had to be changed. For the crew this resulted in a division in the driver's and fighting compartments and an increased thermal load because of the forward position of the engine, further disadvantages of this configuration.

These arguments, which had decided the position of the turret during the design of the *Löwe*, were also applicable in this case. Krupp and *Wa Prüf* 6 also agreed that because of the vehicle's low speed, the type and tuning of the suspension, whether leaf spring or torsion bar, were of secondary importance.

For the planned rail transport of the vehicles, the Army Ordnance Office compared three possibilities against one another. The first proposal envisaged the use of the special flatcar developed by the Simmeringer Waggonfabrik of Graz for the Porsche *Maus*. The car weighed 80 tons and, loaded with the Krupp *Maus*, only slightly exceeded the national railway's height profile.

The second variant envisaged suspending the tank between two five-axle bogies (with transport extensions). The military had used a similar procedure to transport the 600 mm *Karl* heavy howitzer. This solution, which entailed a carriage weight of 44 to 55 tons, did not exceed the railroad profile dimensions.

The third solution required a ten-axle articulated car with a vehicle weight of 55 tons. The tank would be loaded with the help of hydraulic rams and special side ramps.

It was clear, however, that the Army Ordnance Office could not decide on a transport method until a decision on the vehicle's weight had been made. However, both Krupp and *Wa Prüf* 6 had a major interest in a short-term production of the 143-ton Krupp *Maus*, which because of its proven *Tiger* components could be put into production immediately. The project was under time pressure, however; through his statements to Hitler, Professor Porsche had set the time frame: to get the contract, Krupp absolutely had to deliver the first vehicle by autumn 1943. This in turn required an acceleration of the design work, and therefore Kniepkamp suggested that the development of important running-gear components be assigned to MAN *Oberstleutnant* Holzhäuer, department head of *Wa Prüf* 6, wanted to bring about a quick decision by the Tank Committee via *Oberst* Thomale. The conclusion of those at the meeting was that the latter was more in favor of the Krupp *Maus* than the Porsche *Maus*.

On December 18, 1942, Krupp outlined the possible ways of reducing weight from 170 tons (drawing W 1671) to 143 tons (drawing W 1677):

1. Deletion of the outer 3.93-inch armor protection
2. Reduction of the thicknesses of the rear wall, roof, and floor
3. Narrowing of the tank enclosure by about 11.8 inches to 128 inches, by using transport tracks during rail transport. No blocking of two-way traffic as with a vehicle width of 145 inches.

The transport cradle for the *Gerät* 40 (600 mm howitzer)

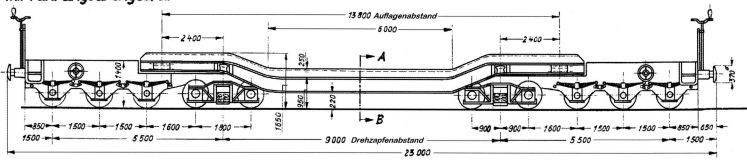

10 achs. Tiefladewagen mit Führungsdrehgestell

The ten-axle depressed-center flatcar with lead truck by LHW Breslau. *Deppmeyer Collection*

The Advantages of the Krupp Maus
■ Steering ration 1:1.5 compared to 1:2.5
■ No blocking of two-way traffic
■ No blocking of running gear caused by dirt buildup
■ Proven components, immediate series production
■ Lower weight, therefore higher production rate and lower materials and fuel requirements

4. Reduction of turret wall thickness by 10 percent
5. Use of weaker *Tiger* components
6. Shortening of the track contact area by 35 inches and the tank enclosure by 27 inches, resulting from the weight decreases in points 1 to 5[7]

By December 31, 1942, Krupp presented a number of design drawings of the Krupp *Maus*, which by then was also called the *Tiger Maus*, in which the decision between drawings W 1686 and W 1677 was ultimately the most important. Krupp envisaged that the first Krupp *Maus* would be delivered by November 1943.

■ Drawing **W 1677**: 143-ton vehicle with light track protection and heavy side armor
■ Drawing **W 1686**: heavier track protection on the front and sides and lighter side armor

■ Drawing **W 1679**: barrel overhang of the *Tiger* and *Tiger Maus*
■ Drawing **W 1681**: 143-ton vehicle with turret moved to the rear
■ Drawing **W 1687**: weight calculations

Despite this, on January 3, 1943, Hitler decided in favor of the Porsche *Maus*. As a result, the designs for the *Tiger Maus* initially disappeared into the archives, only to be brought back out about three weeks later.

Henschel also designed an *Über-Tiger*, which, with a total weight of 99 tons, had an 88 mm *Kampfwagenkanone* with a length of L/71 in a 21-ton turret. Ammunition capacity was sixty rounds, including sixteen rounds in the turret. Powered by a Maybach HL 230 twelve-cylinder gasoline engine combined with a mechanical transmission. The running gear, which weighed 21.6 tons, had thirty-two road wheels with a diameter of 27.5 inches, which ran on a 39-inch-wide track. Crew was to have consisted of six men.

CHAPTER 2
From the *Tiger Maus* to the E-100 Tank

On January 26, 1943, *Diplom-Ingenieur* Kniepkamp, head of the research department of *Wa Prüf* 6, retrieved the weight table for the VK 7001 with *Tiger* assemblies and 88 mm turret. Starting in June 1943, on this basis he and his staff worked on a template for the development of a new series of armored vehicles that were to enter service in 1944–45. Frontline experience also flowed into the project, as did experience with assemblies and components already in production. Because *General* Emil Leeb, head of the Army Ordnance Office, had placed a development ban on his administration on May 17, 1942,[8] Kniepkamp gave the existing design plans and documents on the *Tiger Maus* to companies that had never before produced tanks and had absolutely no experience in this field. Kniepkamp could thus allow his ideas to flow into the project without officially violating the design ban.

All designs shared the larger interior while retaining the external dimensions and weights. To achieve this, the torsion bar suspension, which had proved itself but which required large quantities of materials and space, had to be removed from the fighting compartment. The second measure, planned for all but the heaviest type, banished the previously separate drive components such as transmission, steering transmission, and turret drive with the associated Cardan shaft and reduction gear from the fighting compartment. *Wa Prüf* 6's plan envisaged these elements as being located in the rear of the tank as a compact propulsion unit, so that the entire unit could be replaced if repairs or the replacement of assemblies became necessary. This not only reduced work time but also provided more room for ammunition, enabled the fitting of larger weapons, and reduced overall height. It also created the possibility of installing a floor hatch, something the units had been requesting for a long time. This vitally important emergency opening was present only on the *Tiger* II tank and the *Jagdtiger* heavy tank destroyer. Material standardization assumed a very important place in the planning, because

Wa Prüf 6 tried to use as many parts as possible that were already in production.

A Completely New Series with Many Identical Parts

The designs for the new generation of tanks were basically conventional, although the external mounting of the running gear, promoted by Kniepkamp, was new and would be a part of all future developments. While extremely effective and providing very good driving characteristics, the torsion bar suspensions previously used were expensive to produce and maintain, had a high material cost, and resulted in increased overall height because the torsion bars passed through the fighting compartment.

The high cost of repairs also placed a heavy burden on the repair units. These disadvantages ultimately led to the planned use of external suspension units, which, except for the heaviest class, consisted of disc spring packets. This suspension unit had been designed by Professor Dr. Lehr as an enclosed, encapsulated group at the beginning of 1944. The new program comprised proposals for various weight classes.

Type E-5, Class from 5 to 10 Tons (5.5 to 11 Metric Tons)

This was the plan for versions of the small tank destroyer, scout tank, and light personnel transport vehicle. It was conceived as a two-man vehicle, primarily for the parachute

Wooden model of the *Rutscher* tank destroyer with two 80 mm PAW

troops. The Army Ordnance Office specified an armament of one 80 mm antitank rocket gun. According to *Oberst* Holzhäuer, approximately twenty designs were created, including

- ■ a design by BMW for the 3.5-ton Rutscher tank destroyer equipped with two 80 mm antitank rocket guns (PAW) and with a length of 11.6 ft.,
- ■ a design by Büssing NAG for a VK 501 vehicle weighing 3 tons and powered by a 90 hp Tatra four-cylinder diesel engine,
- ■ a design by Weserhütte AG as Project VK 301, and
- ■ a design for a two-seat tank destroyer by Klöckner-Humboldt-Deutz, which was to use existing components.

All these projects were rejected by the military on account of their lack of armor protection and weak armament.

Type E-10,
Class from 10 to 15 Tons

Planning autonomy was officially with Klöckner-Humboldt-Deutz in Ulm, at the Magirus factory. This company's only previous tracked vehicle was the *Raupenschlepper Ost*

RSO/03, whose components this project was to build on. Proposed versions included an armored troop carrier and a light tank destroyer with a crew of three. The project used the running-gear components of the larger E-25. The Army Ordnance Office envisaged the 75 mm *Panzerabwehrkanone* 39 L/48 as the vehicle's main armament. The design used external suspension elements based on disc springs, to which four road wheels would be attached on each side. The project was abandoned because the design of the *Jagdpanzer* 38(D), successor to the *Jagdpanzer Hetzer*, had proved superior.

Type E-25,
Class from 25 to 30 Tons

Planning was carried out by Argus in Frankfurt (Main) for a vehicle to replace the tank destroyers based on the *Panzer* IV. The result was an interim solution that fell between the *Jagdpanzer* 38(D) and the *Jagdpanther* tank destroyer. To provide the best possible protection, the vehicle had a low silhouette with sloped armor on all sides, similar to that of the *Hetzer* tank destroyer. To better exploit the interior space, external suspension elements were used. Five externally mounted spring plate suspension units were present on each side, with interleaved road wheels. Tracks, road wheels, and

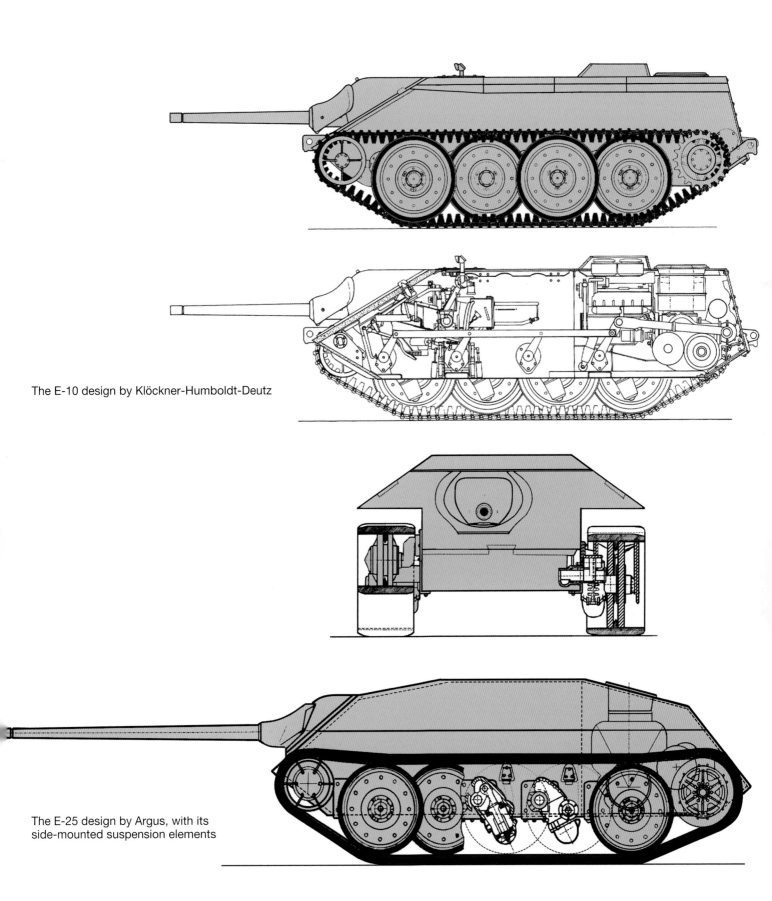

The E-10 design by Klöckner-Humboldt-Deutz

The E-25 design by Argus, with its side-mounted suspension elements

drive sprockets came from the *Panzer V Panther*. Each road wheel had a suspension element with spring plates and hydraulic shock absorbers. The spring housing moved with the road wheel, while the associated crank arm was attached rigidly to the hull. Contrary to usual German practice, the drive sprocket was in the rear, even though *Wa Prüf* 6 believed that the front drive system offered clear advantages because of the better self-cleaning of the tracks and a more favorable center of gravity resulting from the distribution of assemblies. The drive system, consisting of engine, transmission, cooling system, and steering transmission, formed a compact unit that could be removed as a whole. For the new propulsion

concept the company wanted to use the 400 hp Maybach HL 100, a transversely mounted engine producing 400 hp that was still under development, or an air-cooled Argus gasoline engine producing 350 hp, with a Voith hydraulic torque converter and hydrostatic-steering transmission. Power transfer between the gearbox and steering was achieved by planetary gears and the drive sprockets located behind them. *Wa Prüf* 6 envisaged the 75 mm *Panzerjägerkanone* L/70 as the vehicle's main armament. According to unconfirmed sources, several completed hulls were transported from Kattowitz to Alkett Berlin for completion of assembly.

The Rheinmetall design of July 29, 1943, armed with a 105 mm field howitzer

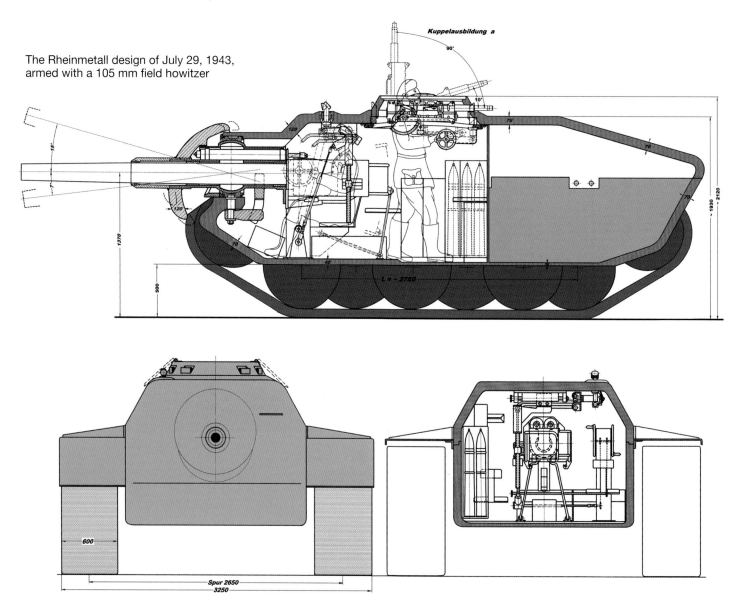

Rheinmetall-Borsig

Also in this weight class were several independent developments, such as the heavy small tank with a 105 mm *leichte Feldhaubitze* 43 (light field howitzer) and a 30 mm MK 108 antiaircraft cannon, manufactured by the company Rheinmetall-Borsig AG of Düsseldorf in July 1943. It had a small turret that had to be opened to fire the automatic cannon. Weighing 127 lbs., the MK 108 had been used very successfully as an aircraft weapon and had an electropneumatic cocking-and-extraction system. The shell casings were not ejected, instead remaining in the belt. Rheinmetall-Borsig

was able to increase the initial rate of fire of 600 rounds per minute to 900 to 1,000 rounds per minute. The crew of four had an ammunition supply of forty-four rounds of 105 mm ammunition and 700 rounds for the 30 mm cannon. The two-part armored superstructure was cast armor with 4.7 inches of frontal armor and 2.75 inches on the sides, the roof, and the rear. Floor plate thickness diminished from 1.6 inches forward to 1.2 inches at the rear. Weight was supposed to be 27 tons. The vehicle had a turning ratio of 1.04 and a ground pressure of 11.37 psi. It had a low silhouette, with

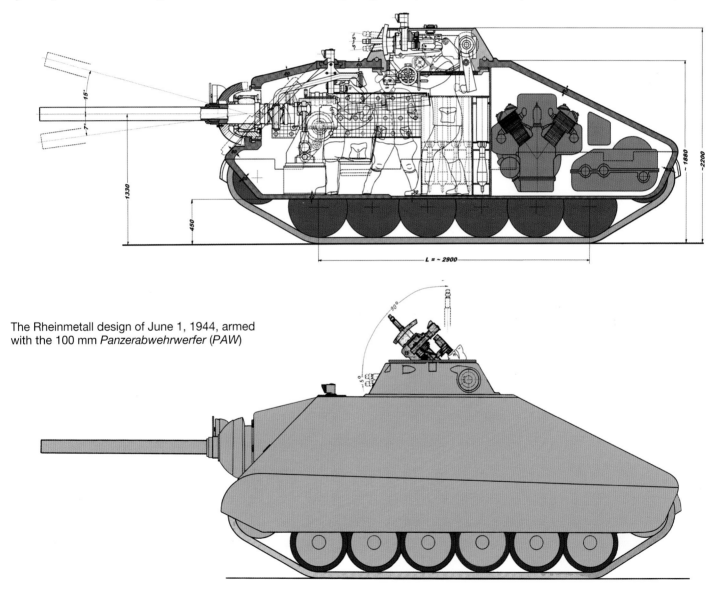

The Rheinmetall design of June 1, 1944, armed with the 100 mm *Panzerabwehrwerfer* (*PAW*)

an overall height of 86 inches and a width of 126 inches. Firing height of the 105 mm gun was just 54 inches.

A design produced by the company in June 1944 showed a very advanced heavy small combat vehicle with a 105 mm antitank rocket gun and a 30 mm MK 108 antiaircraft cannon, plus an "infrared search device" and rangefinder. Its gross weight was 26 tons, and it had a steering ratio of 1:16 and a ground pressure of 11.37 psi. The planned antitank rocket gun achieved a muzzle velocity of 2,800 fps with a projectile weight of 13.5 lbs. In cartridge form, the 37-inch-long ammunition weighed about 22 lbs. Ammunition supply was sixty-five rounds. The two-part cast superstructure had 3.15 inches of frontal armor, while the lower front, the rear, and the roof had 2.55 inches of armor. The sides and forward floor armor were 1.6 inches thick. The armor was sloped all around, improving its effectiveness.

The running gear was covered by 0.8-inch skirts. A width of 124 inches and a height of 86 inches produced a very compact vehicle with a low silhouette; firing height was 52 inches, even lower than that of the design described previously. The four-man crew used elbow telescopic sights so as not to weaken the frontal armor. The antitank rocket gun's gunner also had an FG 1250 night vision device, consisting of a 7.9-inch searchlight with infrared filter defusing lens and infrared telescopic sight, coupled with the telescopic sight. In addition, a power generator would have had to be installed, along with a transformer and vibrator. The horizontal 47-inch rangefinder was in the turret, however, and had to be operated separately. The turret gunner could fire on ground targets under armor protection. Only for air defense did the turret gunner have to fire with the turret top open. The vehicle was to have been powered by a twelve-cylinder diesel engine of "V" configuration. It was to have been produced by Porsche from the ten-cylinder Porsche 101/3 A.

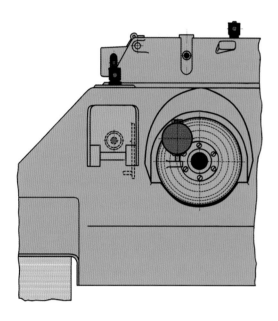

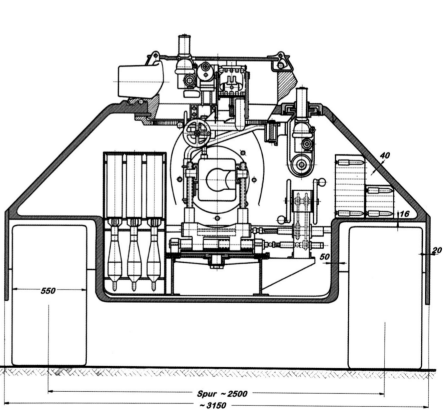

The Porsche Designs

Porsche KG also produced independent designs within this weight class in July–August 1943. Under the heading *Sonderfahrzeug* V (Special Vehicle 5), Porsche designed a light, multipurpose tank (Porsche type 245/1), a light tank (Porsche type 245/2), and a multipurpose tank (Porsche type 250/255), none of which progressed further than the drawing board.

The type 245/1 weighed 19.8 tons. Professor Porsche envisaged an armament of one 55 mm automatic cannon, which because of its large possible elevation could be used both against ground and air targets. The three-man tank was powered by a type 101 air-cooled ten-cylinder gasoline engine made by Porsche. This version of the 300 hp engine from the Porsche *Tiger* was supercharged and produced

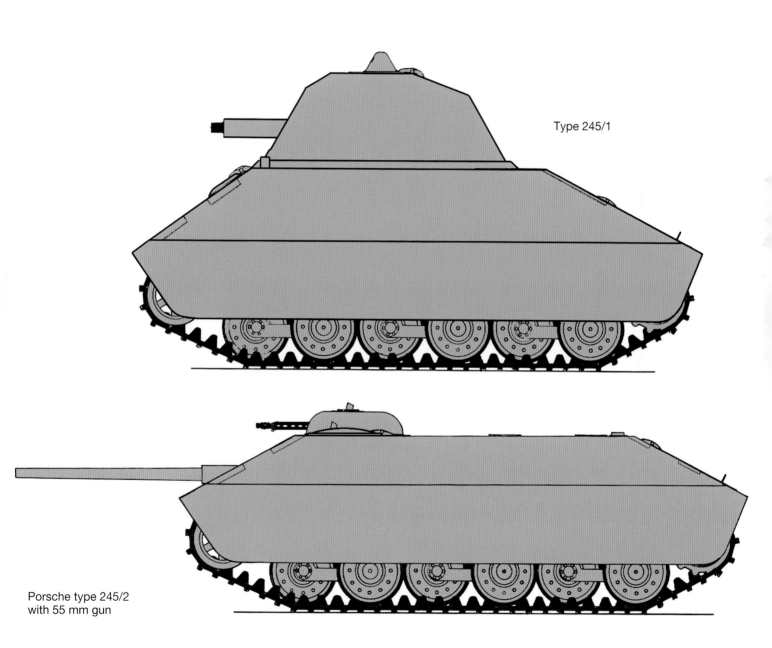

Type 245/1

Porsche type 245/2
with 55 mm gun

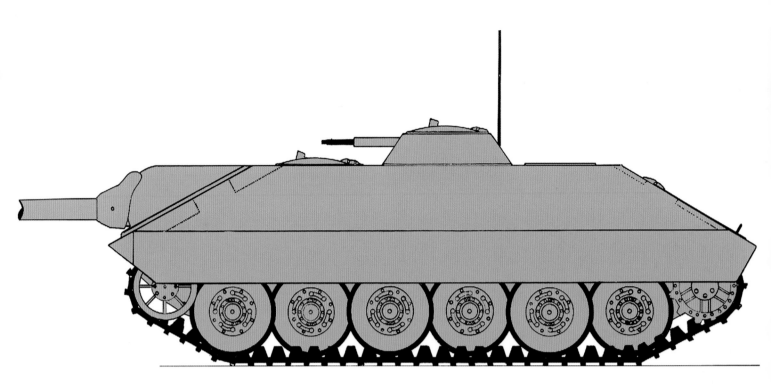

Porsche type 250/255 with 105 mm gun

345 hp at 2,500 rpm. Power transfer took place by means of a hydraulic converter, which was supposed to allow a maximum speed of 40 mph. The running gear followed the suspension principle of the *Maus* tank, with its volute spring suspension. Forward armor consisted of a 2.4-inch plate.

The second project was an assault gun with a crew of two, which was based on the same design. This vehicle weighed 16.5 tons and was armed with a longer version of the 55 mm gun with limited traverse and a firing height of 44.5 inches. The crew also had a 7.92 mm machine gun in a turret. Despite this, vehicle height was just 57 inches. Porsche had envisaged using the Maybach HL 116 gasoline engine, producing 250 hp, and again with the help of a Voith torque converter it would be capable of a top speed of 36 mph. The choice of engine may have been a concession to *Wa Prüf* 6. Armor protection was similar to that of the 245/1; the longer gun increased overall length to 235 inches.

Porsche designated types 250 and 255 as "Special Vehicle VI." These considerably larger vehicles differed only in their power transfer systems, either mechanical (type 250)

or hydraulic (type 255). The design closely resembled Rheinmetall's and was probably the result of joint development. Similar to an assault guns, this design also weighed 29.75 tons and had 4.7 inches of frontal armor. The Porsche engineers also used the 105 mm gun and the 30 mm automatic cannon (both from Rheinmetall-Borsig). Porsche envisaged a developed version of its air-cooled twelve-cylinder gasoline engine derived from the ten-cylinder type 101. With a displacement of 18 liters (1,100 cubic inches), the transversely mounted power plant produced 500 hp, which was supposed to give the vehicle a top speed of 35 mph. The type 250 with mechanical gearbox had a gross weight of just 27.5 tons. The suspension again consisted of the familiar volute springs, supporting three roller carriages on each side. The crew consisted of four men. Unlike the Rheinmetall design, the vehicle had a 13.75-ton welded hull and thinner 1.75-inch side armor. Professor Porsche proposed Krupp as the manufacturer, but ultimately this advanced project also got no further than the drawing board.

Types E-50 and E-75, Classes from 50 Tons and 75 to 80 Tons

These two designs, which were supposed to replace the *Panther* II and *Tiger* II, were essentially identical and differed only in armor thicknesses. The Army Ordnance Office selected the companies Adler of Frankfurt (Main) and Weserhütte of Bad Oeynhausen as contractors. Both types were to have identical hulls that differed only in armor thickness and thus weight. The E-50 hull weighed about 44 tons, whereas that of the E-75 was supposed to weigh 66 tons. The E-50/75-80 class had one bogie with disc springs for each two road wheels. This suspension system, also called the Belleville Washer Suspension, was based on a plurality of aligned groups of uniform Belleville springs. The resulting spring force is equal to that of a single spring. The E-75, however, had two additional road wheels on each side to deal with its greater weight.

Typical features of both tank hulls included reinforced forward floors and more heavily armored entry hatches, intended to improve resistance against mines. *Wa Prüf* 6 had planned to equip both types with identical battle tracks, an identical cooling and fuel system, and an identical drive unit. This drive unit consisted of a supercharged Maybach HL 232 gasoline engine, which was still under development and promised to deliver 1,000 hp, or a Maybach HL 234 gasoline engine, with an output of 900 hp, combined with a hydraulic eight-speed preselector gearbox from the same manufacturer and a double-radius cross-drive steering transmission. These assemblies were to be combined into a single component, with an expected weight savings of 2,200 lbs. and a 23 percent reduction in time required to manufacture the vehicles. Maintenance costs were expected to drop just as significantly. For the E-75 the company planned an additional gear reduction to compensate for its higher weight.

On the running gear, the encapsulated spring units were to accept two independently sprung rubber-saving (solid steel) road wheels. The road wheels were mounted on crank arms, inside of which was a gear segment. These segments transmitted the wheel load to internal horizontal-toothed racks. These rested on differently rated disc springs with a diameter of 7.3 inches. For the heavier E-75 the designers used additional 3.9-inch disc springs. The company attached the hydraulic shock absorber's casing to the other side of the toothed rack. Oil for the shock and vibration absorbers was supplied by the vehicle's central lubrication system. *Wa Prüf* 6 planned a maximum speed of 37 mph for the E-50 and 25 mph for the E-75.

The *Wa Prüf* 6 research department also envisaged an 88-ton assault guns based on the E-75 tank as a replacement for the *Jagdtiger* tank destroyer. Exactly what the turret would look like had not yet been defined, though it was certain that the turret would be driven by an electric motor. An auxiliary system would provide the necessary power, making it possible to traverse the turret even when the main engine was off. This also had the advantage that the turret traverse system operated independently of main engine revolutions and was also more fire resistant, because the highly flammable hydraulic fluid was absent.

As can be seen in the drawings, the suspension elements closely resembled the Porsche bogies used in the *Tiger (P)* and *Jagdtiger (P)*. Their design and operation were also very similar; consequently it is no wonder that these similarities have led to mix-ups in the literature on the subject.

Little is known about the design of the turret. Krupp was responsible for the design work and envisaged either an 88 mm or 105 mm gun. It is conceivable that the so-called *Panther-Schmalturm* (*Panther* narrow turret) with *Saukopf* mantlet, then under testing for the E-50, could have been planned, since it had the most-modern components of the day, such as an Em 1.32 m R horizontal rangefinder and an elbow telescopic turret sight. It was also planned that the turret could be stabilized horizontally. The Army Ordnance Office had also made preparations for the installation of the FG 1250 night-driving and targeting system. The turret had a narrow but more heavily armored front plate, with a thickness of 4.7 inches. This narrow turret's side armor was 2.35 inches thick. The coaxial MG34 machine gun was replaced by the more reliable and faster-firing MG42, in part because production of the MG34 was running down.

The turret shown here was fitted with a developed version of the 75 mm KwK 44/1 from Skoda, with no muzzle brake,

Einheitslaufwerk für E 50/E 75

E 50 (Firma Adler)

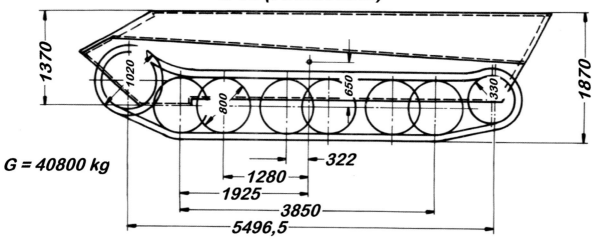

G = 40800 kg

E 75 (Firma Adler)

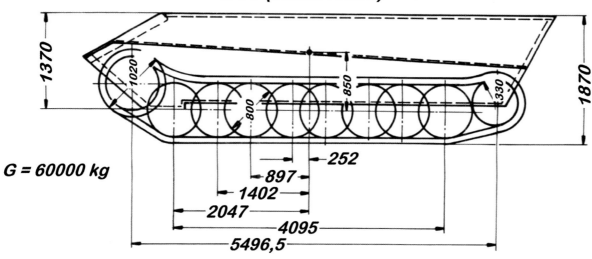

G = 60000 kg

E 75 (Weserhütte)

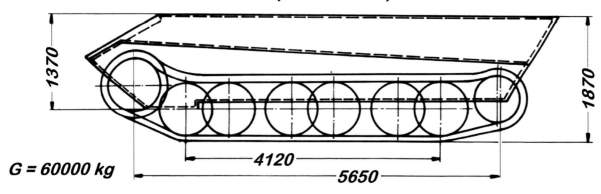

G = 60000 kg

The planned vehicle dimensions of the E-50/75 series

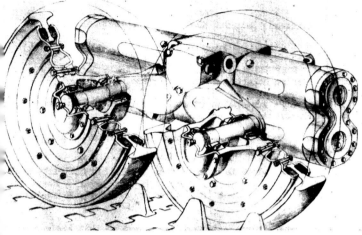

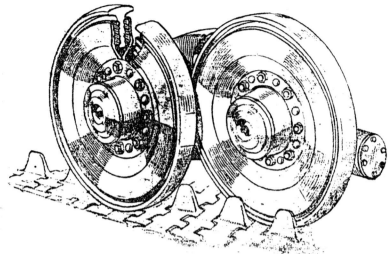

Both variants used interleaved so-called "rubber-saving" road wheels. *Left*, the plate spring bogie; *right*, the Porsche bogie from the *Tiger (P)* and *Jagdtiger (P)*.

Design of the plate spring elements of the E-50/75

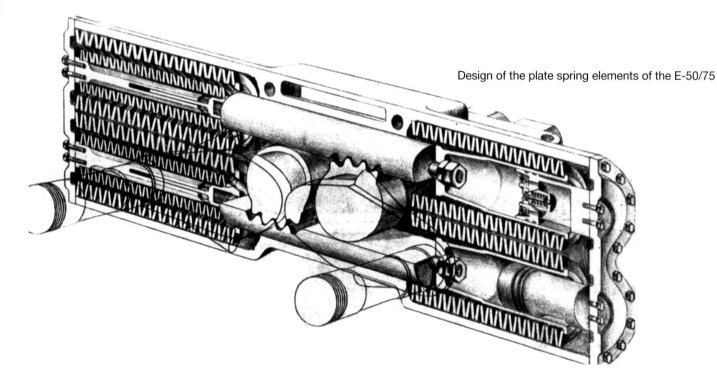

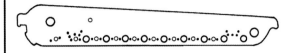

HENSCHEL

Wannenbearbeitungszeit	360 Stunden
Kosten für die dazu benötigten Werkzeugmaschinen	RM 866 000,–
Rohmaterialgewicht der Federungsteile einschl. Stoßdämpfer	17 200 kp
Gewicht dieser Teile bearbeitet	9 480 kp
Aufwand an Maschinenarbeit für Federungsteile einschl. Stoßdämpfer	460 Stunden

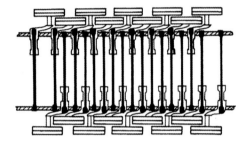

Um einen Kurbelarm zu entfernen ist es notwendig, auch die nebenan liegenden Räder auszubauen.
18 Drehstäbe, jeder 1960 mm lang mit einem Fertiggewicht von 887 kp.
Zentralschmierung für 36 Schwingarmlager.
Größtes Schmiedestück (Schwingarm) 200 kp.

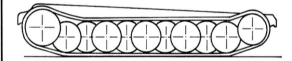

PORSCHE

Wannenbearbeitungszeit	140 Stunden
Kosten für die dazu benötigten Werkzeugmaschinen	RM 462 000,–
Rohmaterialgewicht der Federungsteile einschl. Stoßdämpfer	12 000 kp
Gewicht dieser Teile bearbeitet	6 800 kp
Aufwand an Maschinenarbeit für Federungsteile einschl. Stoßdämpfer	230 Stunden
Einsparung im Gewicht	2 680 kp
Einsparung an Kosten für Werkzeugmaschinen	RM 404 000,–

Es ist möglich, einen Rollenwagen auszubauen ohne andere Teile ebenfalls ausbauen zu müssen. Auch wird keine Winde benötigt. Alle Schraubverbindungen sind von außen zugänglich.

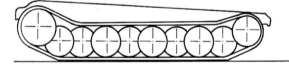

The similarity of the suspension elements suggests a comparison of the spring plate design with the torsion bars used by the *Jagdtiger*.

because the sabot ammunition then in development could not yet be built for use with a muzzle brake. The sabot ammunition had the advantage of high muzzle velocity and thus greater kinetic energy for penetrating the thickest armor. The designers exploited the recoil energy to blow out the powder gases with the help of an additional cylinder beneath the gun. The otherwise necessary compressor was eliminated. A narrow turret design by Krupp with an 88 mm KwK L/71 as used in the *Tiger* II tank survived the war. As can be seen in the drawing, this turret would have been fitted with an Em 1.6 m R armored turret rangefinder, which because of turret width needed a different base.

The so-called *Schmalturm* (narrow turret) with *Saukopf* mantlet

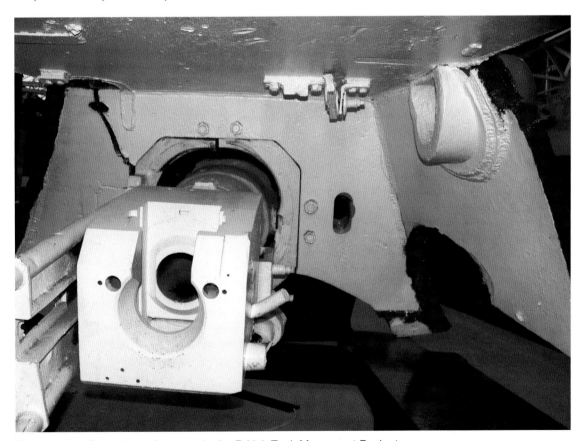

The surviving *Schmalturm* fragment in the British Tank Museum at Bovington

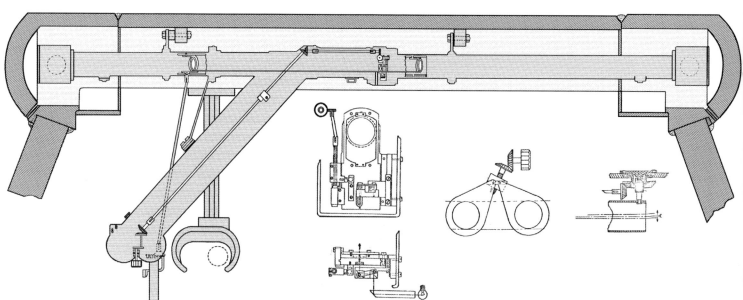

Tank turret: *Em 1,6 m R (Pz.)* Rangefinder

Type E-100, Class from 130 to 140 Tons

This type was envisaged as a solution for the *Maus* tank. On June 30, 1943, the Adler company, under the leadership of Director Jensche, was invited to develop a tank in this weight class. *Wa Prüf* 6/F specified as basic parameters, on the basis of the Krupp *Maus*, a gross weight of about 154 tons, which was to comprise the 88-ton hull with removable track protection and the 56.75-ton *Maus* turret plus accessories and equipment. The track contact surface of 192 inches, combined with 39-inch-wide battle tracks, resulted in the relatively high ground pressure of 20.3 psi, which was roughly similar to the ground pressure (without sink depth) of the 208-ton *Maus* I. Because of the curved shape of the track links, the effective track width of the E-100 project without sink depth turned out to be somewhat less and was roughly equivalent to that of the 21.7-inch-wide transport tracks. The reduction in turret weight, which will be described later, was therefore in particular an important step in the right direction. The overall length of the tank with the 150 mm KwK L/36 was 403.5 inches.

The dimensions of the hull were 335 inches in length, 176 inches in width (with spaced armor), and 130 inches in height, including turret. Ground clearance was 22.4 inches. The armor plate thicknesses were 7.9 inches for the upper bow plate, which was sloped 30 degrees, and 4.7 inches for the lower bow plate, sloped at 45 degrees. The vertical side plates were 4.7 inches thick, and it was possible to add spaced armor up to 2.95 inches thick. The rear plate, which was sloped at 68 degrees, was up to 5.9 inches thick. The forward hull floor was 3.35 inches thick and thus offered excellent protection against mines. The floor tapered after about 78.75 inches, and at the rear the armor thickness was about 1.6 inches.

Weak Point: The Engine

The power plant once again proved a source of problems. Use of the 1,200 hp Maybach gasoline engine favored by Kniepkamp with a new MEKYDRO mechanical-hydraulic eight-speed transmission was supposed to result in a top speed of 25 mph. But this Maybach gasoline engine did not exist. To achieve such a performance, this engine would have had to be mechanically supercharged with mechanical fuel injection based on the HL 230. Because of the shortage of suitable materials, however, the engineers could use such exhaust gas turbosuperchargers only with diesel engines because of their lower exhaust gas temperatures. The new Maybach HL 232 engine produced a maximum of 1,000 hp at 3,000 rpm, and under existing conditions it was not possible for Maybach to achieve an output of 1,200. There was just a single prototype of the Maybach HL 234 gasoline engine, which with mechanical fuel injection produced 900 hp at 3,000 rpm.

Since Maybach could not complete these HL projects in time, *Wa Prüf* 6 decided to install *Tiger* II components, with the 700 hp twelve-cylinder Maybach HL 230 P45 gasoline engine, the Maybach OG 401 216 B OLVAR transmission, and the Henschel L 801 twin-radius-steering transmission. With this system even the 77-ton *Tiger B*, with a power-to-weight ratio of 10.1 hp per ton, was underpowered; purely theoretically, the 140-ton E-100 project would have been capable of just 14.3 mph with the same power plant. Power-to-weight ratio would have been a completely unsatisfactory 5 hp per ton. By comparison, the final version of the *Maus* tank by Porsche, with the 1,200 hp diesel engine, at least had a power-to-weight ratio of 6.35 hp per ton, which was also insufficient. The E-100's fuel capacity was to be 317 gallons, distributed between a main tank holding 224.5 gallons and another 92.5 gallons in the auxiliary tanks in the engine compartment.

The Running Gear

Unlike the lighter types previously described, instead of the disc spring per swing arm and road wheels, the E-100 was to have two coil springs and front drive, previously standard in German tank design. The reason for this was probably the turret ring diameter of 118 inches, since with a longer engine compartment the turret would have moved too far forward. The Maybach 1,200 hp gasoline engine would also have required greater radiator space.

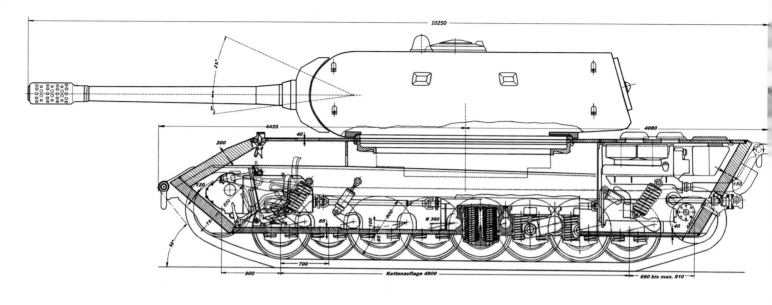

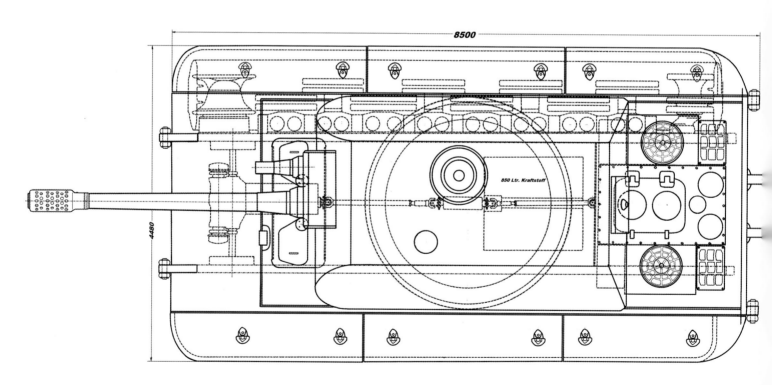

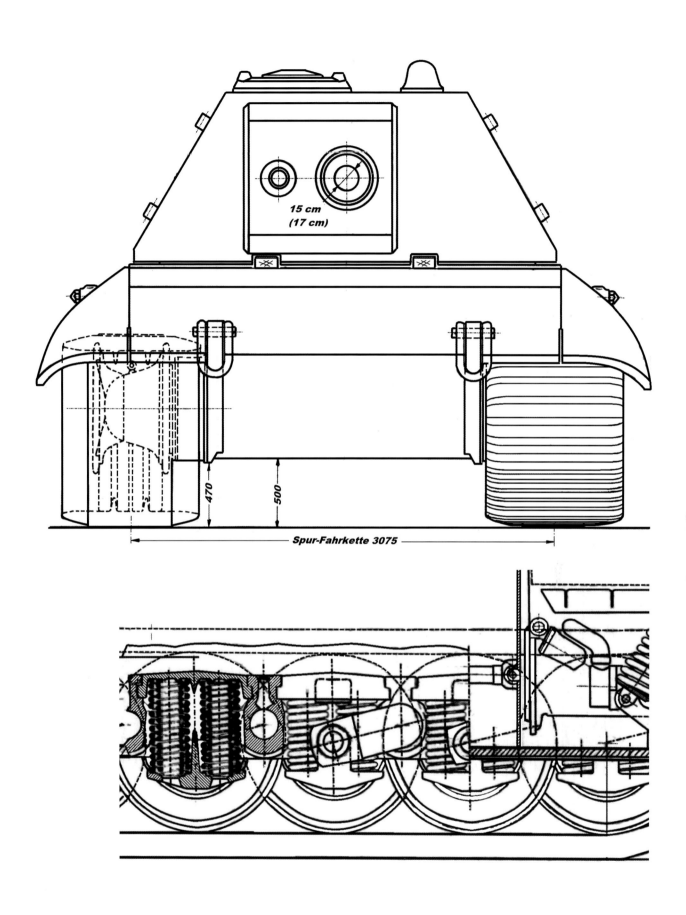

15 cm
(17 cm)

470

500

Spur-Fahrkette 3075

The road wheel crank arms with hubs for the 35-inch road wheels. Behind them are the plate springs of the coil spring pairs, which have not yet been mounted.

A Clear Case of Copyright Infringement

By incorporating features of the Krupp *Maus* design into the E-100, Undersecretary Kniepkamp of course antagonized the Krupp company. This is expressed so clearly in a memo by *Oberingenieur* Wolfert, manager of Krupp Artillery Designs (AKP), about a meeting at the Kummersdorf firing range on May 30, 1944, that it is worth reproducing the original text: "At a meeting with Undersecretary Kniepkamp about further development of the E-100, Kniepkamp offhandedly declared that the design of our *Tiger-Maus* from November 1942 was going to form the basis of the E-100 and that only the running-gear suspension would differ. After the decision in favor of the Porsche-*Maus* at the end of 1942, Kniepkamp had also picked up our project again in spring 1943 and had received permission from *Oberst* Holzhäuer of the tank committee to build an E-100 experimental vehicle as part of his (!) development series of experimental tanks. I took the view that it would have been a good idea to approach AK, the intellectual creator of this project. Development of the chassis and turret by a company with many years of experience in both fields would certainly have been more advantageous

than in the current time, repeatedly bringing in new companies, irrespective of the complicated combination of different companies. Kniepkamp claimed that in his view, AK was overburdened with other work. I replied that we had sufficient designers and could certainly have found a way for a quick solution. Kniepkamp still expressed concerns that FK [Krupp] did not have a capable and mobile experimental workshop for tanks. I pointed out the experimental workshop at G.w.k."

Undersecretary Kniepkamp played down the issue, and his position was almost unassailable. The companies to which he had given the new projects, with no experience in building tanks, were dependent on him and more easily influenced. But Erich Woelfert did not give up. The next day, on the occasion of a demonstration of the *Heuschrecke IVB* (Grasshopper) self-propelled gun, he commented that "I also made *Oberst* Holzhäuer [head of *Wa Prüf* 6] aware of our cooperation with Adler on the chassis of the E-100. Apart from the running-gear suspension, the current E-100 was completely based on the design submitted by us in November 1942, the *Tiger-Maus*. Production of the first prototype vehicle, especially the development of the chassis and turret, could certainly be accelerated considerably by using a company with experience in both areas. It was my impression that *Oberst* Holzhäuer had not been properly informed by Kniepkamp, since he initially believed that the E-100 was fundamentally different than our *Tiger-Maus*. I was, however, able to convince *Oberst* Holzhäuer that the opposite was true."

Woelfert spared no effort. He subsequently spoke with *Oberst* Crohn, head of the Tanks Main Group at *Wa Prüf* 6, and informed him of the conversation with *Oberst* Holzhäuer and Ernst Kniepkamp. However, "Crohn wanted nothing to do with Kniepkamp and his development vehicles, but he insisted that we verify our authorship of the E-100 in writing by sending drawings to *Oberst* Holzhäuer."[9]

This entire squabble suggests that the construction of the E-100 had not been officially authorized, especially because it violated Hitler's development ban of May 1944. *Oberst* Crohn knew that, but he was also aware of Kniepkamp's great influence on the head of *Wa Prüf* 6, *Oberst* Holzhäuer. He in turn was a willing tool of State Secretary Saur of the Armaments Ministry. Thus, all the participants must have been aware of the narrow path they were treading.

Further Development despite the *Führer*'s Ban

On May 22, 1944, during an armaments conference at *Führer* headquarters, Hitler approved a decree that banned the development of new weapons and equipment, as well as changes to those that already existed. It again materialized at the Berghof on July 6, 1944: "From the current situation the *Führer* orders the cessation of all developments of armored vehicles with heavy and very heavy guns. He requests only the accelerated presentation of a design for a self-propelled carriage for the 170 mm gun based exclusively on elements of the *Tiger*."[10]

Despite this, Undersecretary Kniepkamp had the Henschel company's Tank Experimental Station 96 at Haustenbeck (near Paderborn) construct a prototype of the chassis for the E-100 tank. Kniepkamp had already successfully put into practice his *Tiger* I project with this company.

Arrival of the E-100 hull shell at the *Panzerversuchsstation* 96 in Haustenbeck

The numbers shown in the map legend also appear in the following photo captions.

Haustenbeck

Panzerversuchsstation 96 Haustenbeck

Brinkmann Nr. 86

Legend:

1. Residential building with canteen and recreation room
2. Residential tract for station employees
3. Station manager
4. Visitor accommodation
5. Gas pumps
6. Small plunge pool
7. Workshop
8. Corrugated hall
9. Air raid shelter
10. Hall with 16.5-ton crane
11. *Tiger* Hall
12. Garages
13. Workshop
14. Large plunge pool
15. Pump shacks with hoses to plunge pools
16. Dam for dammed-up Rote Bach (red brook)
17. Gas hall

Zufahrt zum Erprobungsgelände

Waldweg zum Aschenweg

Skizze: Walter Göbel

The tank hull on wooden blocks in the *Tiger* Hall (Hall No. 1) at Haustenbeck

The 60-ton "production turret," as used on the *Panzerkampfwagen Maus*

demanded by Hitler. The reason for the slow work pace was surely also the uncertainty about the main armament. With the *Maus* turret mounting the 128 mm KwK, already in production, the tank was more than 55 tons too heavy. Kniepkamp therefore concentrated on the 128 mm turret for the *Maus* II, which was about 17.5 tons lighter. A wooden model was being prepared at the Kummersdorf range. Both turrets were equally well suited for the use of a 150 mm KwK.

In the chamfered face of the lighter 35-ton turret, the 75 mm gun was above the main armament rather than to its right, similar to the Rheinmetall version of the *Neubaufahrzeug*.

The redesigned turret front enabled the *Wa Prüf* 6 to eliminate the lower shot trap and also reduce weight considerably. Armor thickness was not supposed to exceed 7.9 inches (instead of 9 inches) in the front plates, 3.1 inches (instead of 7.9 inches) on the sides, 5.9 inches (instead of 7.9 inches) in the rear, and 1.6 inches on top (instead of 2.5 inches). The

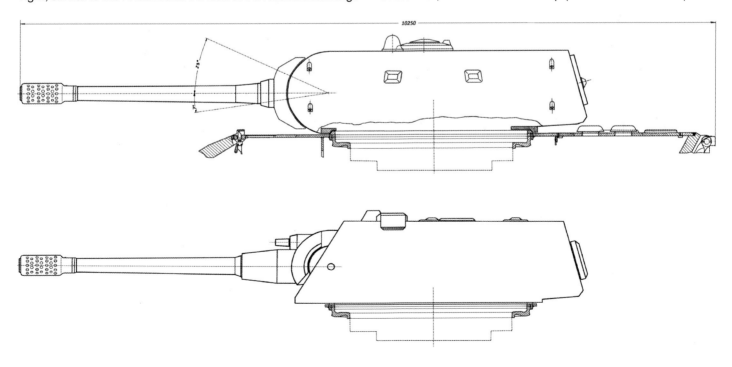

A good view of the turret ring armor, which has been milled to the maximum extent possible

research department had also envisaged a horizontal rangefinder for this new turret, similar to that in the previously mentioned "narrow turret." This could have reduced the vehicle's operational weight from 154 to about 136 tons.

The turret ring diameter, as previously mentioned, was 118 inches. This diameter was the result of the gun recoil at all barrel elevations and the length of the ammunition. This caused enormous problems in the E-100, since the external hull width was just 124 inches. The side armor was therefore milled out to achieve the required diameter.

The use of larger-caliber guns with greater recoil and longer ammunition was thus excluded from the outset. The 170 mm gun being discussed could be used only with a fixed assault gun superstructure; however, work on the 150 mm / 170 mm assault gun based on the E-100 was halted by order of the Army Ordnance Office. Porsche had also received a development contract for a "15/17-cm *Sturmgeschütz auf Mausfahrzeug*" (150 mm / 170 mm assault gun on *Maus* vehicle) on May 17, 1944, although Krupp-AK pointed out the greater height of the *Maus* vehicle compared to that of the E-100 project. This would inevitably have led to an exceedance of the railroad profile, and the 30 mm flak

turret planned by Porsche would have hindered the man gun's barrel recoil.[11]

However, use of the favored 150 mm KwK L/38 had to be abandoned on June 5, 1944; a letter from Krupp to the armaments representatives reveals that the two *Maus* guns with muzzle brake, including the five replacement gun barrels, were no longer needed, and there was no longer any interest in the production of these barrels.[12]

Most likely this was due to the problems in reloading the large-caliber ammunition in the cramped fighting compartment. The 150 mm L/4 antitank round weighed 99 lbs., but the *Wa Prüf* 6 had known this since the trials with the smaller 128 mm ammunition were conducted.

State of the Project in January 1945

On January 15, 1945, Engineer Arnoldt sent a final report on the E-100 to *Diplom-Ingenieur* Jaeger of the Army High Command, to Adler, and to Kniepkamp, head of *Wa Prüf* 6/F.

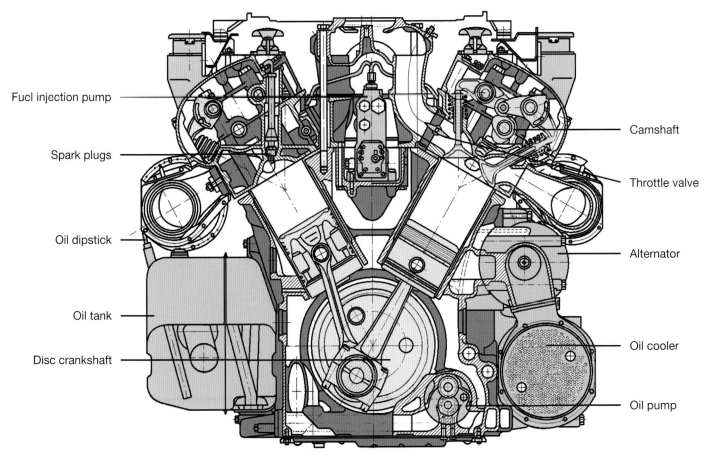

Fuel injection pump

Spark plugs

Oil dipstick

Oil tank

Disc crankshaft

Camshaft

Throttle valve

Alternator

Oil cooler

Oil pump

The Maybach HL 234 engine with mechanical fuel injection, which was supposed to produce 900 hp, proved to be unstable. Because of this, it later had to be restricted to 850 hp.

Illustrated with sixty-four photos, it described in detail the structure of the completed hull.[13]

This document is also exemplary of the rapidly deteriorating war situation, since it had often not been possible to obtain the parts needed for building the hull in time. Despite everything, the three Adler employees had their hands full. As an example, Engineer Arnoldt wrote that the coil springs had still not arrived due to misdirection of the railcar carrying them. The same was true of the two battle tracks.

The transport tracks, however, had already been stored at the experimental station in Haustenbeck. Assembly of the parts located between the bulkhead partition and the rear wall had been completed apart from the still-missing fuel lines. Henschel had, however, still not delivered the cover plate over the transmission. Regardless, a test run of the engine would be possible after delivery of the missing fuel lines and completion of the electrical system, As previously described, the power plant would be neither the 1,000 hp Maybach HL 232 gasoline engine, promised for 1943, nor the 900 hp Maybach HL 234 gasoline engine, but rather the 700 hp HL 230 with OLVAR transmission and steering control, which was insufficiently powerful.

To improve the problematic exhaust temperatures, installation of an additional cooling fan, the so-called "John" ventilator, was envisaged. This had already been tested on a *Tiger* II at Haustenbeck. It was supposed to eliminate flames spurting from the exhaust, which gave away the tank's position in darkness. The cooling fan drew the necessary air from the intakes for underwater travel in the center of the grating.

When Engineer Arnoldt wrote his report, the questions concerning the turret and the size of the ballast weight

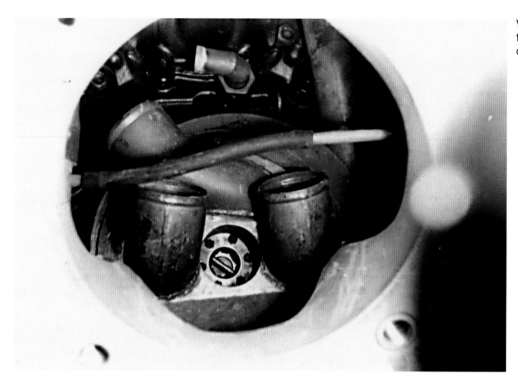

View of the "John ventilator" through the large opening in the rear of the E-100

remained unanswered. Since a new design was impossible in the existing situation, the partly complete 55-ton turret (56.75 tons with ammunition) would have had to be used. With a planned vehicle weight of 154 tons, the hull with track shields accounted for 58 tons; the engine and accessories, 6.6 tons; the running gear, 22 tons; and accessories and equipment, 10.5 tons. With the less powerful engine, top speed would at best have been 14.3 mph. Sprung weight was supposed to be 141 tons.

The steering ratio—the ratio of track width to track contact surface—was 1:1.6. In comparison, the *Maus*, with its allegedly "nonsteerable" ratio of 1:2.53, was very easy to steer. With tracks 39 inches wide, the track contact area of 15,190 square inches yielded the previously mentioned ground pressure of

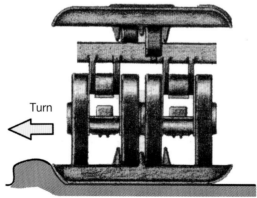

Turn

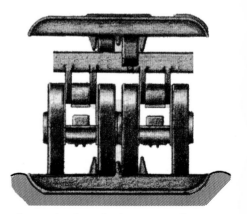

Smaller track contact area on hard ground without sink depth, 1.45 kg/cm²

Slight pushing away of the ground during a turn

Larger track contact area on soft ground with 4-inch sink depth, 18 psi

Comparison of different track contact areas on the basis of the example of the *Maus*

The supplementary side armor of the E-100 discarded in the open

20.3 psi, which was comparable to that of the 189-ton *Maus* tank without including sink depth (with the sink depth of the 43-inch-wide tracks, the *Maus* achieved 18.06 psi).

In addition to the space-saving external spring suspension, the chassis of the E-100 had several improvements compared to the *Tiger* II series. Another innovation was the removable spaced armor for the tracks. This auxiliary side armor could be installed and removed by the crew with the help of a crane, without outside assistance. Carrying racks were envisaged on the sides of the turret.

This supplementary armor would have protected the 4.7-inch-thick vertical flanks with additional 2.9-inch-thick spaced armor plates. Krupp AK had carried out firing trials at the company's firing range at Meppen on November 22, 1943, using a 128 mm L/62 study barrel mounted on a 210 mm *Mörser* 18 carriage. Fired from a range of 590 ft., none of the six 128 mm armor-piercing *Panzergranaten* 43 rounds could penetrate the 6.7-inch-thick armor. The 1.2-inch-spaced armor, installed 11.8 inches from the main armor, caused the premature detonation of four shells, so that when

they struck the 6.7-inch main armor behind it they had already burst. The other two shells broke up on the second plate and destroyed the explosive charge. In comparison, the approximately 0.2-inch-thick armored skirts, standard on other tank types, were intended mainly to protect against the Russian 145 mm antitank rifle and possibly against lower-velocity high-explosive or hollow-charge shells. Such thinner-spaced armor had no significant effect on full-caliber or subcaliber solid-shot rounds.

While the side armor of the *Maus* tank was 7 inches thick, this spaced armor on the E-100 was removable, to avoid exceeding railroad load weights.

Like the *Tiger*, this was also true of the 39-inch-wide battle tracks, the outer road wheels, and, unlike the *Tiger*, the external gear rims of the drive sprockets and the outer halves of both idler wheels. This was a clear disadvantage of the E-100 project, which after unloading would have to be placed in battle condition, while the *Maus* could be used immediately. As well, carrying battle tracks, wheels, and spaced armor would have required additional transport space.

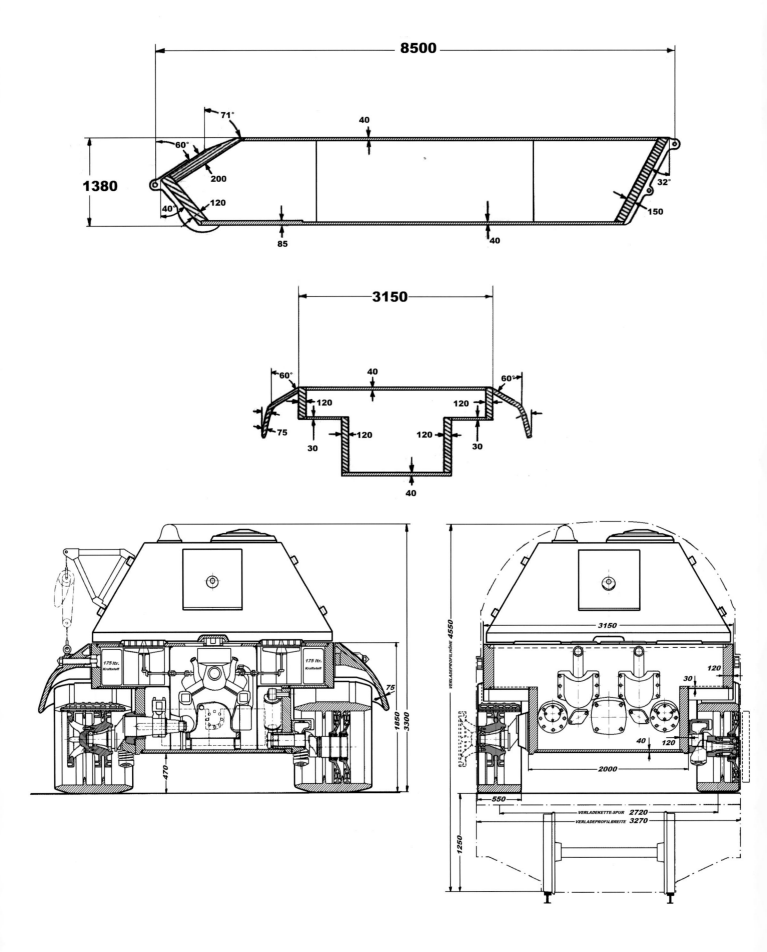

8500

1380

71°

60°

200

120

40°

85

40

40

32°

150

3150

60°

40

60°

120

120

75

120

120

30

30

40

175 ltr.
Kraftstoff

175 ltr.
Kraftstoff

75

1850

3300

470

VERLADEPROFILHÖHE 4550

3150

120

30

40

120

2000

550

VERLADEKETTE-SPUR 2720

VERLADEPROFILBREITE 3270

1250

50

The E-100: An Interesting Experimental Vehicle

In the end the E-100 was an interesting experimental vehicle that lacked a suitable power plant and turret. Its tactical potential was similar to that of the *Maus*, which was a mobile "bunker" with severely limited operational capabilities. It was, however, lighter than a *Maus* tank, had a lower profile, and consumed fewer materials and took less time to produce, since many components had been used in the *Tiger*. Nevertheless, the *Maus* tank had advantages over the E-100. The *Maus*'s underwater capability and gas defense system had been dealt with constructively, and it had an auxiliary engine to generate power for the turret traverse when the main engine was shut down.

The engine question had not been satisfactorily resolved for either type and would not be for years to come. The planned twelve-cylinder Maybach HL 295 engine with integral auxiliary engine, also gasoline powered, was supposed to replace the 1,000 hp Maybach HL 232 gasoline engine. It did not become production-ready until after the war, in the late 1940s, with French help. At the time it had been recognized that the highly developed gasoline engine had little future in tank design on account of the fire danger, high fuel consumption, and limited range.

Developed by Maybach employees in France, the 1,000 hp Maybach HL 295 gasoline engine with the HL 11 auxiliary engine in the center. The engine was very heavy, weighing 26.5 tons. The financial costs of a private development, as would have been necessary with this engine, were too great.

The Haustenbeck Testing Station

On April 2, 1945, American troops occupied the area around Haustenbeck and examined all the vehicles there. The captured vehicles and documents were of such importance to the occupiers that Engineer Arnoldt and his coworkers had to continue their work at the Americans' behest. The E-100's hull was to be completed, since the engine with radiators and cooling fans had been removed because of the absent fuel lines. As the accompanying view of the *Tiger*

This view of the hull from the right front shows the reduction gearing, which has not yet been bolted in place, with mounted drive sprocket. The teeth are missing, as are the coil springs. Visible above is the welded-on pickup points for the side-spaced armor.

These views of the left side show the same level of completion.

The interleaved road wheels, 35 inches in diameter, have been partially mounted. Despite the very different method of mounting the road wheels, the hubs and road wheel crank arms look identical.

The upper spring bases for the coil springs can be seen in front of the idler wheel in the foreground.

A good view of the separable idler wheel on the right idler wheel crank arm.

In addition to the covers over the track-tensioning mechanism, this overall view of the rear hull also shows the cover for the inertia starter. The studs above were envisaged for the armored exhaust pipe covers.

The hanging running-gear swing arms and the lower plate springs for the yet-to-be-installed coil springs attached to them

The hull openings in the floor of the E-100 in detail

a and b: access to the internal parts of the idler-wheel-tensioning system
c: access to the water drain valve
d: access to the water pipes
e and f: access to the floor valve (planned)
g: access to the threaded fuel drain plug (planned)

The closed engine cover with the mushroom-shaped armored intake covers

The open engine cover reveals the Maybach HL 230 P 45 gasoline engine's air filter housing.

The right intake grate in opened and closed positions. In the center is the air extraction fan blade. Because of the tank's underwater capability, these spaces on the outside were also called the "overflow area."

View with the rear engine cover removed. At the top left is the fuel-filling tank, and next to it, on the right, is the water-filling tank.

The center engine compartment openings for fuel:

a: extraction point to the John ventilator
b: fuel-filling point
c: coolant-filling point

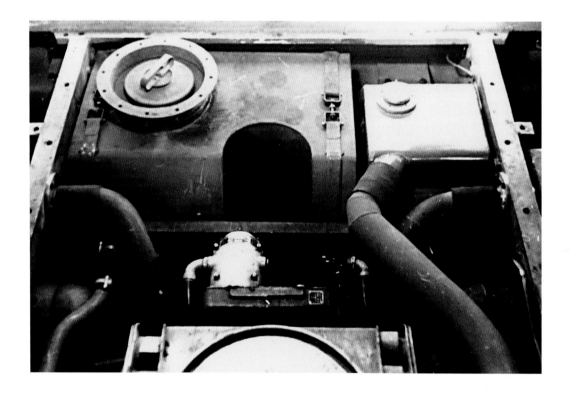

This view shows the rear part of the Maybach HL 230 gasoline engine with the magnetos. The magneto on the left, in the direction of travel, is missing.

All engine covers have been removed, revealing the water hoses and the air filters.

The suction pipes and water hoses of the cooling system. In the center of the photo on the left, the oil-filling point of the right fan drive.

The rearward view from above, through the turret circle opening toward the bulkhead between the engine and fighting compartment. One can easily imagine how much space the turret with its 118-inch turret ring occupied. Below, left and right of the Cardan shaft, was the central fuel tank.

Close-up views of the areas to the left and right of the tank, showing the two 12-volt batteries and their heating plates (for winter operation). On both sides one can see the caps over the swing arm mounts for the road wheels.

As on all German tanks, an important control panel was located on the bulkhead in front of the engine compartment. Mounted on it is the switch panel, with various switching devices.

Switch panel on the bulkhead partition:

a: electric automatic fire-extinguishing system by Minimax
b: opening to the engine compartment and the fuel shutoff valve
c: fuel starter pump
d: Cardan shaft to transmission
e: air channels to the exhaust pipes
f: exhaust valve rotary valve
g: floor valve

Details of switch panel on the bulkhead partition:

a: switch (contacter) for the starter (2 × 12 volts = 24 volts)
b: main battery switch (main circuit breaker)
c: warning-light suppressor
d: alternator voltage regulator
e: alternator suppressor
f: 12-volt socket for the hand lamp

View from the rear looking forward. The front part of the fighting compartment, with cover for installation and the transmission and steering control removed.

The fighting compartment with the 225-gallon fuel tank. The hydraulic turret drive was located here in the *Tiger* II. This could be done away with in the E-100, since an electric turret drive with separate power source was envisaged. Analogous to the *Maus* tank, the designers used the Leonardo principle, a simplified system in which a low-voltage electric motor drove a high-voltage generator. This generator supplied power to the traverse motor via the regulating switch of the turret traverse system.

Front left, the covered Cardan shaft leads toward the transmission. In contrast to the *Tiger* II series, at the front the E-100 had two shock absorbers per side. In this photo the driver's seat is in the lowered position.

The sheet-metal transmission cover with suction tube on the left. On the right side the radio operator's seat is missing. No bow machine gun was envisaged because of the homogeneously strong armor protection. The hose on the floor on the right led from the bulkhead partition to the instrument panel.

View from above, showing the foot pedals, the steering wheel, the emergency steering lever, and the covered Olvar transmission next to the driver's seat. The gear preselector lever is located on the right. Above right in the photo is the steering gear with the Argus steering slide housing mounted on it.

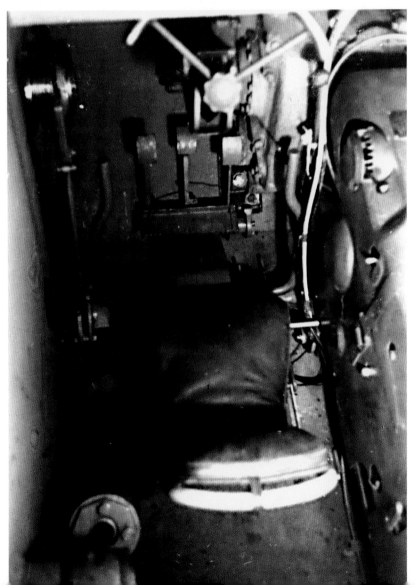

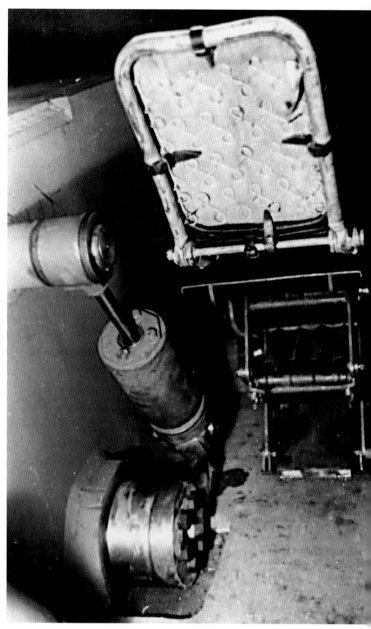

Once again the different seat positions for normal travel and combat. Above the steering wheel is the cutout for the folding driver's periscope.

II's fuel system shows, all assemblies had to be removed in order to connect the fuel tanks. That is why the American occupiers found the E-100 hull in this disassembled condition.

A total of seven tanks had to be connected, with auxiliary tanks in the engine compartment on the floor and in both radiator compartments. The fuel supply system consisted

The E-100 hull as discovered by the Americans in the so-called *Tiger* Hall.

There is no discernible construction progress on the suspension compared to the report from January 1945.

By the time the Americans arrived, the fitters had removed the power plant, including fans and radiators.

of three circuits, which according to H-DV 656/43 were to be emptied in the following sequence:

■ engine compartment auxiliary tank: tank under left cooling fan, 21.1 gallons
■ engine compartment main tanks: tanks in engine compartment to the left and right of the engine; the filling container on the rear wall and under the right cooling fan; 116 gallons
■ fighting compartment: two 45-gallon tanks in the *Tiger* II, in the E-100 replaced by a single 225-gallon tank

Since the total fuel capacity was given as 317 gallons, the tanks must have been smaller because of a planned larger cooling system.

A number of captured German armored vehicles, including *Jagdtiger* 323 in the hands of the French, were repaired at the station. The British took over this area in the summer of 1945 and were thus responsible for the station. They too were interested in the experimental station continuing its work. Among the captured vehicles, in addition to the E-100 tank and the *Grille* 17 self-propelled gun, were two *Tiger Bs* with Porsche turret, a *Jagdtiger* heavy tank destroyer with Porsche running gear, a VK 3001 (H) tank with a ballast

View of the E-100's hull from the crane hall (*10*) looking toward the workshops. On the right are the vehicle's tracks.

The E-100 seen from the rear. In the background is the *Tiger* Hall (*11*), through which the pump shacks (*15*) and the large plunge pool (*14*) could be seen. Next to it, on the left, are the garages (*12*), and on the right are the workshops (*13*), in front of which is the *Mörserlafette* 18 with 210 mm gun barrel. On the far left is the slanted roof of the crane hall (*10*).

The hull as seen from the roof of the crane hall. The fitters have completed installation of the road wheels, and the off-road tracks lie ready for installation; only the transmission cover with driver's and radio operator's hatches is missing. The workers placed all possible accessory parts in the hull for transport.

The design of the 1,000 mm wide off-road tracks is reminiscent of the two-part *Tiger* II tracks with additional cleats on the main and intermediate links. The latter consisted of three parts.

The spaced armor pieces seen from the inside. The track in the foreground is the narrower transport track. Both parts probably stayed at Haustenbeck for scrapping.

weight in place of a turret, a *Tiger* I tank, a *Panther* tank, a prototype of the DW I tank, and a Soviet KV-I. The vehicles were positioned on the open area of the so-called *Tiger* Hall (11), where they were photographed and filmed. Firing and submerged driving experiments were also carried out with the *Tiger* I.

The test station remained in operation until the end of 1945. The most-interesting vehicles, such as the E-100 hull, the *Jagdtiger* (305 004), a *Tiger* II with Porsche turret (V2), the *Tiger* I, and other armored vehicles, were transported to England for testing. The British used the station until September 1946. In the summer of 1948, they blew up the installations in the Sennelager area.[14]

While the other "souvenirs" survived in the museum, after its use as a "hard target" at an unidentified firing range in England, the E-100 hull was probably badly damaged and scrapped.

CHAPTER 3
The 17-Centimeter-Selbstfahrlafette 17/21 Grille 17

With a weight of 64 tons, this was not actually in the superheavy category; however, the E-100 hull was created in the shadow of this self-propelled gun. Using its own resources, in 1942 Krupp produced wooden models of heavy self-propelled guns that later became the *Grille* (cricket) series, based on the *Tiger* and *Panther* chassis. The self-propelled carriages mounting the 170 mm gun and the 210 mm *Mörser* 18 heavy howitzer received considerable support from Hitler at an

The 170 mm cannon in firing position in Italy, 1944. *BA 1011-310-0895-13A*

armaments conference on July 24, 1942, and were ordered to be developed into experimental pieces.[15]

These self-propelled carriages went under the collective name *Grille* 17/21, since the installation of a 210 mm heavy howitzer on the same chassis was also planned. The gun was to be capable both of being fired from the vehicle as well as being removed and fired from a fixed position on the ground. The armor to be used was intended to provide protection against machine gun fire and shell fragments.

The complete breech, gun cradle, bottom gun carriage, pneumatic equilibrator, carriage brake, and recoil mechanism and significant portions of the top carriage and elevating mechanism were to be taken from the 170 mm *Kanone* 18 or the 210 mm *Mörser* 18. The barrel was fitted with a 573 lb. (later corrected to 515 lb.) muzzle brake, which was to eliminate up to 100 percent of the blowback aftereffect. A traversing mechanism at the rear of the top carriage and the top carriage itself were mounted to be rotatable on a slide. Krupp provided the bottom carriage with a foldable trestle. On the self-propelled carriage the gun could fire up to 5 degrees to each side. The vehicle could be positioned to point the gun roughly in the general direction of the target, or it could be driven onto a turntable to allow it to be able to turn 360 degrees. In both cases a trestle had to be folded down and, after each rough traverse, firmly attached to the ground. The 17 cm *Kanone* 44 *(Sf) Geschützwagen* VI (formerly *Gerät* 5-1702 for the 17 cm *K 43 Sf*) had a lengthened *Tiger* hull, initially with the *Tiger* I's running gear and later based on the *Tiger B*.

The interleaved road wheels were sprung with the aid of torsion bars. Of the eleven steel road wheels on each side, nine were bearing road wheels, and there was one raised road wheel at the front and rear. The Maybach HL 230 engine, installed forward of the gun compartment, was separated from the driver's compartment by a double-bulkhead partition. Krupp placed the cooling system and the fuel tanks above the track shields on both sides of the engine. With a sustained output of 650 hp, the engine drove the forward-mounted drive sprockets by way of a Maybach OG 401216 B Olvar transmission, a Henschel L 801 steering transmission, and 900-4 Argus steering brake, plus reduction gear units. ZF had earlier considered the previously envisaged AK 7-200 ZF transmission in combination with the L 801 for the *Panther* II, but like the AK 8-200 it was no longer needed.

The engine compartment had an automatic fire-extinguishing system. *Wa Prüf* 4 had envisaged a BMW engine to start the main engine and keep it warm, but because of supplier difficulties this was later replaced by a standard *Fuchsgerät* engine heater, which could be mounted on the front of the engine from the driver's position. The driver sat on the left and could see out of the hull through a cylindrical lookout with glass prism or by raising his seat. In addition to the Fu-5 radio set (two receivers, one transmitter), the radio operator, seated on the right, also operated the planned bow machine gun. According to *Wa Prüf* 4, however, this machine gun was to be dropped from the production vehicle. Instead, the office envisaged a driver's visor from the *Panther D* tank both for the driver and radio operator.

Krupp had provided the gun compartment with an armored superstructure that had to be folded up for rail transport. For transport, the turntable for the gun at the rear of the vehicle had to be raised with hoists, but for stationary use the gun could be placed on the ground. First, the turntable was removed and the lock between the bottom carriage and vehicle was released. With the help of another vehicle or a winch, the gun was pulled back only so far that the rollers of the bottom carriage were still on the rear of the vehicle. Then the trestle was folded down and bolted to the side of the bottom carriage support. The gun could then be pulled out farther until this support could be locked onto the turntable. Then the vehicle could drive away.

A ground anchor, fire steps, and a loading swing arm were added and the gun was ready to fire. As when firing was occurring from the vehicle, the trestle had to be firmly attached to the ground after every rough traverse setting. The gun did not have to be removed for rail transport; however, the Gg 24-800/300 battle tracks had to be replaced with narrower Gg 24-660/300 transport tracks, the front protective shield had to be folded down, and, after removal of the turntable, the side shields had to be folded.[16]

The vehicle was designed for a crew of eight, which included driver, radio operator, gun commander, and five gunners. Initially the vehicle carried just five rounds of 170 mm ammunition, and only three rounds for the 210 mm heavy howitzer.

		Self-propelled carriage	
Caliber:	170 (210) mm	Chassis:	Krupp based on the *Tiger B*
Caliber length:	L/50 (L/31)	Overall length:	511" (393")
Barrel braking power:	121,254 lbs.	Length of vehicle:	374"
Gun Removed:		Width of vehicle:	124"
Maximum firing range:	18.4 (10.4) miles	Overall height:	124"
Elevation range:	–2° + 48 (–2° + 68°)	Width over outer edge of tracks:	
Traverse range:	360° coarse ± 5° fine	a. 31.5" driving track	141"
Firing position weight:	33,070 (32,188) lbs.	b. 26" off-road track	128"
Stability with maximum charge:	+6°	Track contact surface length:	164"
Firing height:	90.5"	Steering factor	1.5
Overall height:	116"	Specific ground pressure Road:	12.8 lbs./in.^{2}
Gun on Self-Propelled Carriage:		Off-road:	10 lbs./in.^{2}
Elevation range:	–2° + 48 (–2° + 65°)	Ground clearance :	19.6"
Traverse range:	360° coarse ± 5° fine	Fording ability:	27.5"
Combat weight:	132,277 (130,513) lbs.	Climbing ability:	31.5"
Stability with maximum charge:	–2°	Crossing ability:	118"
Firing height:	from caterpillar 91"	Climbing capability:	30°
	from turntable 98"	Maximum speed:	28 mph
Power-to-weight ratio:	11.7 (11.8) hp/ton	Mid-speed on roads:	18.6 mph
Armor:	Bow 1.18"	Off road:	11.2 mph
	Side 0.6"	Range on roads:	155–186 miles
	Rear 0.6"	Range off road:	78–93 miles
	Floor 0.4"	Fuel consumption on roads:	99 gal. / 62 miles
	Roof 0.6"	Off road:	33 gal. / 62 miles

Ballistic Characteristics of the 170 Self-Propelled Gun

Shell Type	Projectile Weight	Muzzle Velocity
Kanonengranate 39	150 lbs.	2,870 fps
Kanonengranate 38 (m. Haube) HL	138.5 lbs.	3,051 fps
Panzergranate L/4.3 (under development)	159 lbs.	2,707 fps
Betongranate L/4.7 (under development)	151 lbs.	no information
Leuchtgranate L/3.7 (under development)	129 lbs.	2,788 fps

Number of propellant charges: 4
Length of casing: 28.5"
Weight of casing: 21 lbs.

Shell Type	Maximum Charge	Weight of Explosive Charge
Kanonengranate 39	64.25 lbs.	16 (10.8%)
Kanonengranate 38 (m. Haube) HL	67 lbs.	13.4 (9.7%)

Penetrative Ability of the *Panzergranate L/4.3*

Range	Impact Angle 60°	Impact Angle 45°
3,280'	10.8"	7.7"
6,561'	9.84"	6.9"
9,840'	8.7"	6.1"

Concerning the ammunition, it can be said that the 170 mm *Kanonengranate 38* with cap became unavailable from mid-1944 onward. As a result, the special charge envisaged for it, the fourth charge, was dropped. The 170 mm gun's first propellant charge consisted of the *Sonderkartusche* 1 (muzzle velocity of 635 meters per second [mps]); the second charge, of the *Sonderkartusche* 1 and *Sonderkartusche* 2 (muzzle velocity of 755 mps); and the third charge, of the main cartridge plus *Vorkartusche* 3 (muzzle velocity 940 mps).

In addition to the fourth propellant charge, the first and second charges for the self-propelled gun were later canceled as well; in addition to the seven projectile baskets, Krupp was able to accommodate seven main and seven forecharge propellant charge containers.

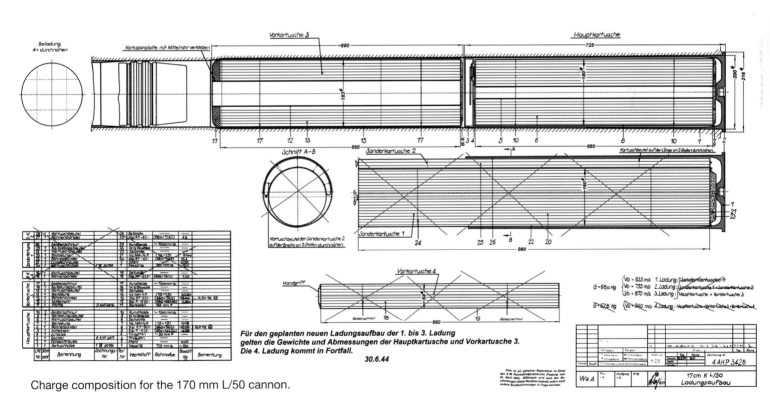

Charge composition for the 170 mm L/50 cannon.

Transport of the ammunition from outside was accomplished with the help of a two-man shell-transporting beam (the 210 mm heavy howitzer used a four-man shell-transporting beam). According to the spec sheet, aiming was accomplished with the 3 × 8 antitank gun telescopic sight. A *Rundblockfernrohr* 36 panoramic sight was also part of the equipment.[17]

In the brief description provided by Krupp on June 25, 1944, aiming equipment was described as "*Zieleinrichtung* 34 for direct fire; for indirect fire this can be switched to alternate targeting system."[18]

Krupp began ordering raw materials at the end of October 1942. Further designs for a wooden model were created in November 1942. On November 9, 1943, Krupp envisaged the priority order for the development contracts, as follows:

- self-propelled carriage *Grille* 17/21 for April 1944
- self-propelled carriage K 4 (mot.) for July 1944
- self-propelled carriage R 2 for September 1944

Krupp planned February 28, 1943, as the completion target for the drawings. Evaluation of the first firing was to take place on August 1, and the final acceptance on September 1, 1943. To keep this schedule, the materials would have to be delivered by the end of March 1943 at the latest. Despite the high priority resulting from the allocation by the Armaments Ministry of special-priority-level "DE" (*dringende Entwicklung*, "urgent development"), the deadline was postponed month by month. Thus, in June 1943 the majority of the pressed, forged, and cast parts were still missing. The constant shortage of the *Tiger* components that were supposed to be used for the hull delayed the planned delivery in autumn 1943. Bombing of the Krupp works in Essen caused another problem, when all the design documents were destroyed in early July 1943. As a result, the design office had to begin the production of documents all over again. This alone increased the number of designer days from 3,500 to 4,500.

The production area budgeted nine-tenths of the roughly 10,000 working hours for production of the *Grille* experimental vehicle. Krupp also required new documents from the many subcontractors, such as Argus, ZF, Maybach, Henschel, Rheinmetall-Borsig, Eberspächter, MAN, Hemscheidt, and Bosch. So, another order for raw materials was placed in December 1943 because, for example, some of the cast

The L/4.3 version of the 159 lb. *Panzergranate* 43 armor-piercing round, December 14, 1944

steel parts could not be delivered by the central foundry until May 1944, at a time that had actually been set as the delivery date for the prototype. On May 25, 1944, the promised completion date was postponed until September 1944. On June 25, 1944, Production Area 10 reported that welding of the hull had been completed.

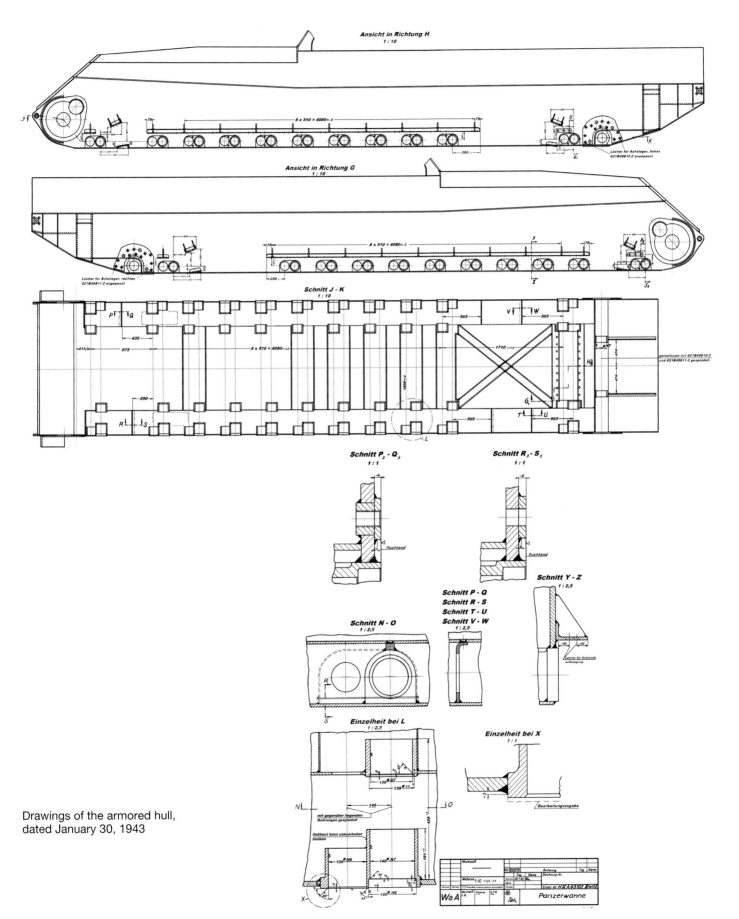

Drawings of the armored hull,
dated January 30, 1943

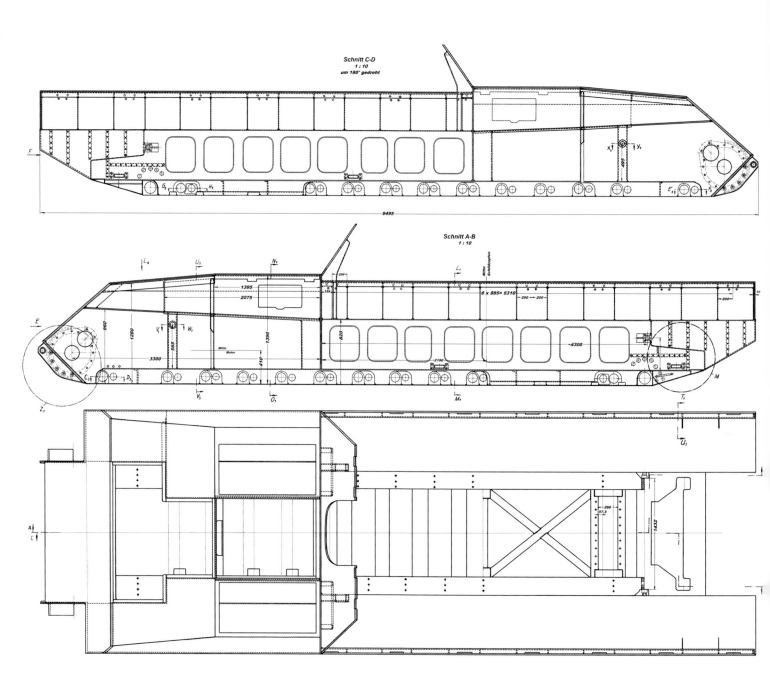

Because of the existing situation, on July 6, 1944, Hitler ordered that all development work on armored vehicles with heavy and very heavy guns was to be stopped. "He demanded only the accelerated presentation of a heavy self-propelled carriage for the 170 mm gun, using *Tiger* components exclusively."[19]

A new problem arose in July, because after two years the DE priority level assigned to the *Grille* had expired. Since obtaining a new designation would take too long through the normal channels, the question arose whether the experimental vehicle could be completed with the normal "SS" priority level. After a discussion on July 26, 1944,

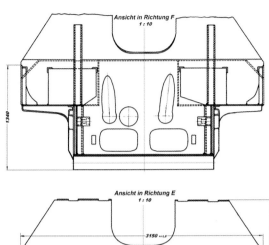

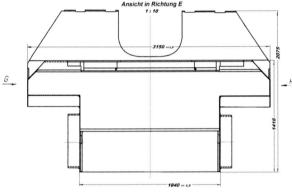

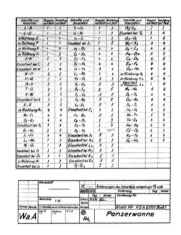

Wa Prüf 4 and Wa Prüf 6 inspected the hull in Production Area 10. During the inspection the representatives of the *Wehrmacht* stated that in the future, two driver's visors from the *Panther* tank should be used in place of the radio operator's mantlet with flexible ball mount and the driver's periscope. As well, the 20 mm cannon previously planned was to be

dropped. Special emphasis was placed on double armoring of the fuel spaces and good sealing between them and the driver's compartment. On the basis of its experience, *Wa Prüf* 6 considered that the total capacity of the six fuel tanks (264 gallons), given an expected fuel consumption of 3.8 to 4.25 gallons per mile, would be inadequate.

Each gun battery was supposed to carry with it an assault gun crane for removal of the engine, if possible with the transmission. The required crane mount was therefore to be welded in place. Furthermore, in addition to the intercom system, a speaking tube was to be installed between the driver's and crew compartments (commander and gunner), since the intercom system in the armored howitzers at the front had not proved totally reliable.

The Army Ordnance Office emphasized that all departments, and the senior command in particular, had great interest in the soonest possible presentation of the experimental unit. The necessity that it be brought forward was particularly stressed. The department promised to take all necessary steps to secure the required vehicle components, on whose timely dispatch the shortening of the construction process depended. In the presence of Dr. Müller, the representatives of the Army Ordnance Office emphasized that the command desperately needed these tank guns.

The manufacture of a large number of these devices could not be justified until the experimental unit had undergone testing; consequently its immediate completion was a compelling necessity. The leadership of *Wa Prüf* 4 awaited a fourteen-day report about the building progress of the experimental unit, since it was under orders to report to the Reich Minister of Armaments and War Production on the production status at fourteen-day intervals beginning on July 27. Materials allocation presented Krupp with an enormous challenge; the problems were a reflection of the time. After repeated reminders from the Army Ordnance Office, the required Maybach HL 240 P30 engine had been delivered to Essen, but because of a misunderstanding it was stored in a maintenance workshop instead of in Production Area 10.

In addition to the Maybach engine, the transmission and steering control, the track drive, the engine for starting and keeping the engine warm, the radio system, and the road wheel cranks were also missing in July 1944. Only parts of the cooling and ventilation system and the side shafts had been delivered. On August 16, *Wa Prüf* 4 sent a letter to

Krupp in which the department complained about the slow construction progress; although the urgency had been stressed at the meeting on July 26, Krupp was giving November 1944 as the completion date. *Wa Prüf* 4 expressed disappointment and drew the conclusion that the date was not being determined by the delivery of vehicle parts but by other influences, whose cause was not known to the department at the time. Therefore *Wa Prüf* 4 again strongly urged that immediate steps were to be taken so that the target date for the presentation could be shortened by four weeks.

On September 13, 1944, *Hauptamtsleiter* Saur turned to Dr. Müller with the request for photographs of the 170 mm gun on the self-propelled carriage, for a *Führer* briefing. Since there were no photographs of the half-completed vehicle, Saur asked if he could at least be sent photos of the wooden model by courier. If this were not possible, a skilled artist could paint a picture of the unit and send photos of it to Berlin. Furthermore, Saur wanted to know the exact delivery date and the extent of the contract; he thought that the date of late November for the experimental unit was too late. In

September 14, he received copies of the only five surviving photos of the wooden model of the *Grille* 17/21, with and without gun enclosure, and the gun in driving position. On September 18, 1944, Krupp again requested that the *Grille* and R 2 project retain its DE priority level. Krupp's request was accompanied by the following information:

- production of the experimental unit: 11,000 hours
- testing and trials: 1,000 hours
- changes after the first service trials: 500 hours
- contract value: target price 85,000 *Reichsmarks*

On September 21, with the aid of drawings and photos of the model 1944, Karl-Otto Saur reported the state of preliminary work for the 170 cm K 72 self-propelled gun based on *Tiger B* components. Hitler ordered that a demonstration should take place as soon as the first experimental unit, then being built, was completed. The deadline given by Hitler was November 1, 1944.[20]

One of the few model photos of the *Grille* 17, here a 1:1 scale wooden model in firing position

The state of the work at that time was as follows:

■ As previously stated, after a lengthy search the engine problems were solved by September 20, 1944.
■ At the instigation of *Wa Prüf* 4, the Olvar transmission, which was received by Henschel on August 9 for the purpose of combining it with the steering control and Argus steering brake, had to reach Krupp for installation by August 31 at the latest. From this resulted the delivery deadline of November 1944.
■ Henschel declined to make delivery of the necessary track drive and referred Krupp to Steyr-Daimler-Puch in St. Valentin. It also saw the track drive as a bottleneck and referred back to Henschel.

The raw and completed road wheel crank arms of the *Tiger*

Not until October 4, 1944, after the inconsistencies had been clarified, were the two track drives finally delivered from the Nibelungenwerk.

■ During the war years the ball-bearing industry occupied a key position, and it is therefore not surprising that the bombing of the center of this industry, Kugelfischer of Schweinfurt, placed the armaments industry in crisis. One result was the halting of *Maus* production, since the twenty-two angular contact roller bearings for the road wheel crank arms had become unavailable.

Since Henschel was unable to provide replacements, consideration was given to procuring them from Sweden; however, with the help of a *Führer* order, the twenty-two angular contact roller bearings were procured from the vicinity of Prague. Some of these, however, were lost during transport.

Procurement of the necessary twenty-two angular contact roller bearings was the high point of the materials problem and mirrored the dilemma of German industry at the end of 1944 very well. Henschel was supposed to deliver the finished road wheel crank arms for the *Grille* to Essen even before the planned delivery of road wheel crank arms in June 1944 for the K 5 (mot.), which was to be made mobile. At the end of June, Henschel informed the Army Ordnance Office and Krupp that it could not deliver the finished road wheel crank arms before September 1944. As replacements for these, at the end of June 1944 Henschel sent twenty-two rough-cut crank arms to Krupp. Since the Krupp factory in Essen was unable to finish these, after clarification on July 21 they were sent to the Krupp-Grusonwerk in Magdeburg. These finished crank arms subsequently went from Magdeburg to Henschel in Kassel on August 30, 1944. Henschel was supposed to apply splines to the crank arms, since Krupp did not think itself capable of doing so. On September 13, Henschel informed Krupp that the crank arms from the Grusonwerk were unusable because they were not sufficiently strong.

Because of the destruction of two of the three production lines, it was impossible for Henschel to divert finished crank arms. The Nibelungenwerk also declined to deliver the items, which were in very short supply. Since Henschel was categorically rejecting the promised delivery of the twenty-two finished crank arms by September, in the interest of meeting the delivery deadline, Krupp considered temporarily installing the crank arms finished by the Grusonwerk so that assembly and preliminary testing could be carried out. Krupp therefore turned to Henschel, requesting that it nevertheless apply the necessary splines to the insufficiently tempered crank arms. Krupp stated that the crank arms had a hardness of 91,030 lbs. per square inch, which was inadequate, but that possibly they could still be used for the Raupenschlepper action.

The crank arms installed in the *Tiger B* (crank arm material 34 CV 7 quenched and tempered) had a strength value of 135,122–156,457 lbs. per square inch. Henschel considered crank arms with a value below 135,122 lbs. per square inch to be rejects, while hardnesses over 156,457 lbs. per square inch created problems working the material, so-called spaces. Since a *Tiger* weighed 77 tons, and the *Grille* just 66 tons, Director Pertus of Henschel was able to imagine driving a *Grille* in the field with the crank arms having a strength value of 91,030 lbs. per square inch. The vehicle would have to be driven with greater caution on paved roads, however. The missing crank arms and the other still-absent parts were picked up in Kassel personally by the dispatch manager of Production Area 10 on October 12, 1944. Krupp wrote to the *Wa Prüf* 4 and Dr. Stieler von Heydekamp, head of the Tank Development Committee, that the experimental unit could be completed on schedule only if *WuG* 6 would take the necessary twenty-two functional road wheel crank arms from *Tiger* production by October 15, 1944.

With reference to the *Führer* order, on October 4 a directive was sent to Henschel for twenty-two road wheel crank arms to be taken from ongoing *Tiger* production. The loss of two *Tigers* from the monthly production total was acceptable in view of the *Führer* order. During a visit by a representative of the armaments ministry on October 4, 1944, Krupp summarized the state of development:

■ Production Area 10 had ended work on the hull by October 6. The covers were 90 percent complete.

■ The engine could be fitted, but it had to be removed again for drilling of the attachment holes.

■ The transmission and steering control were on hand and could be fitted using the holes for the track drives.

■ The lubrication system for the running gear was attached after the engine and transmission were removed for the first time.

- The fuel system was 60 percent complete and fitted. The pipes still had to be attached.
- The hand and foot lever systems, throttle and starter linkage rods, and driver's seat were more than 90 percent complete and fitted.
- The cooling and ventilation systems were complete and have been installed. The associated ducting must still be completed by Henschel and installed.
- Twenty-two road wheel crank arms, which are to be delivered complete, have still not been received. Krupp has requested the twenty-two road wheel crank arms, finished by the Grusonwerk, from Henschel for temporary installation. Of the twenty-two road wheel crank arms, just seven have so far arrived in Essen. A courier is supposed to follow up on the sending and the whereabouts of fifteen more bearings, packed in two crates. As well, four normal torsion bars ordered as replacements from Henschel are still missing. The idler wheel mounting is being worked on; the drive sprockets were twice destroyed. Replacements are being worked on and the tracks are on hand.
- The parts for the electrical system were present in Production Area 10 and were installed after the engine and transmission were removed.
- The armored superstructure could be 95 percent complete; only the joints and supports, including the rods for the support plate (?), remain to be installed.
- The ball mantle for the radio operator's machine gun is ready for installation.
- The inner lining for the 170 mm gun is complete and in storage in Production Area 8. All other parts, including the breech ring and the built-up barrel, are still being worked on.

Krupp named October 20, 1944, as the delivery date. The work on the carriage in Carriage Workshop I was largely complete, and completion of the toothing of the elevation mechanism was planned for October 20. Workers in the production area had welded the support plate with revolving section, and it only had to be bored and spindled by October 10.[21]

Wa Prüf 4 had fixed November 20, 1944, as the deadline for test firing of the gun at Meppen, which was to be followed by checking the fit of the gun in the by-then-completed chassis. On November 20, the unit was to be sent to Hillersleben for testing. Since the gun was fitted with a muzzle brake for the first time, *Wa Prüf* 4 anticipated a fourteen-day testing period. Provided no major problems were encountered, the unit could be demonstrated to Hitler sometime after mid-January 1945. Extensive driving and firing trials would have to be put off until then. *Wa Prüf* 6 considered the use of the tempered road wheel crank arms, even if only for assembly purposes, unacceptable. In the view of *Wa J Rü* (*WuG* 6), the missing parts should be taken from a completed vehicle or from spare parts.

Because of the production of other devices, during a meeting with *Oberst* Wöhlermann of *Wa Prüf* 4 on October 9, 1944, a list was made of the necessary parts. He also read out loud a letter from Reich Armaments Minister Speer dated September 25, 1944, according to which experimental devices were to be shown to the *Führer* immediately after their completion, and the production of at least two devices per month was to be begun as quickly as possible. Since the end of November had been named in all the fourteen-day reports submitted to Speer about the completion date of the experimental unit, Wöhlermann wanted Krupp to tell him when the experimental unit would in fact be complete, provided all parts were available. The *Oberst*, however, rejected the idea of showing the device to the *Führer* without previous testing.

There were doubts that even if the gun could be fired a few days after November 20, the complete vehicle could be finished before the end of the month. Krupp agreed that at least eight days would be required for the final mounting of the gun on the vehicle, and the initial firing and driving trials at Meppen. It was decided that an inspection would take place at Essen, so that, including the time for transport, another fourteen days would be needed so that the unit could be ready for official trials at the end of the year. Provided there were no special circumstances or transport difficulties, the unit could be available for presentation by mid-January 1945.

The Krupp representative made it clear that the necessary running-gear parts had still not arrived from Henschel. *WuG* 6 requested a list of the missing parts so that it could ensure that

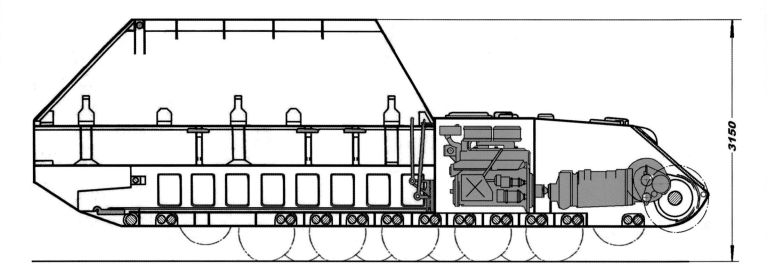

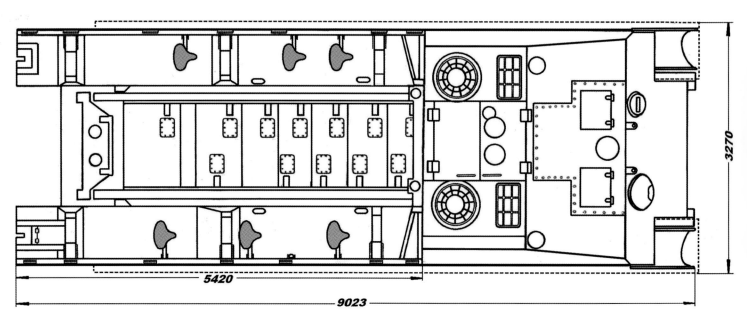

The cross-section drawing of the chassis of the *Geschützwagen* VI, here still with the ZF transmission. The vehicle was intended to mount either the 170 mm cannon or 210 mm howitzer.

they were immediately taken from ongoing production. Upon questioning, *Diplom-Ingenieur* Jaeger of *Wa Prüf* 6 stated that he thought that it would be possible to drive slowly with the untempered road wheel crank arms. It was clear to *WuG* 6 that production of such a special hull on an existing *Tiger* production line such as the ones at Henschel or the Nibelungenwerk was not possible, since this would result in the loss of at least ten *Tiger* hulls. *Oberst* von Wilke did, however, see as possible the diversion of sufficient *Tiger* components for two units per month from ongoing production.

So, according to *Oberst* von Wilke, that left only Krupp for the production of two hulls per month, especially since Krupp was the only choice for production of the 170 mm gun. Hanomag, the second manufacturer of these guns, had recorded serious interruptions in production because of "enemy action"; consequently, the two guns produced each month could come only from Krupp. Of course, this could be only at the expense of the 170 mm field gun produced there. Krupp agreed under the condition that all parts be delivered on time. The necessary production documents were available.

On October 11, after visiting Henschel, *Major* Koch of *WuG* 6 declared that Henschel would not be in a position in the near future to deliver tempered road wheel crank arms, and therefore the untempered road wheel crank arms would have to be installed. Dr. Müller rejected this in his letter of October 17 and declared that if the tempered road wheel crank arms were not available within eight days, he would

have to report this to the Armaments Ministry and the Tank Main Committee, since this made it impossible for him to meet the stated deadline for completion of the experimental unit; after delivery of the crank arms, Production Area 10 would need about five more weeks for final completion of the vehicle. *WuG* 6 was also supposed to determine whether the necessary tempered road wheel crank arms could be taken from production at the Nibelungenwerk, since the finishing of the crank arm blanks was not possible at that time, neither by Henschel nor by the Grusonwerk. The Armaments Ministry had meanwhile given Krupp an extension of the *Grille* 17's priority level until April 31, 1945.

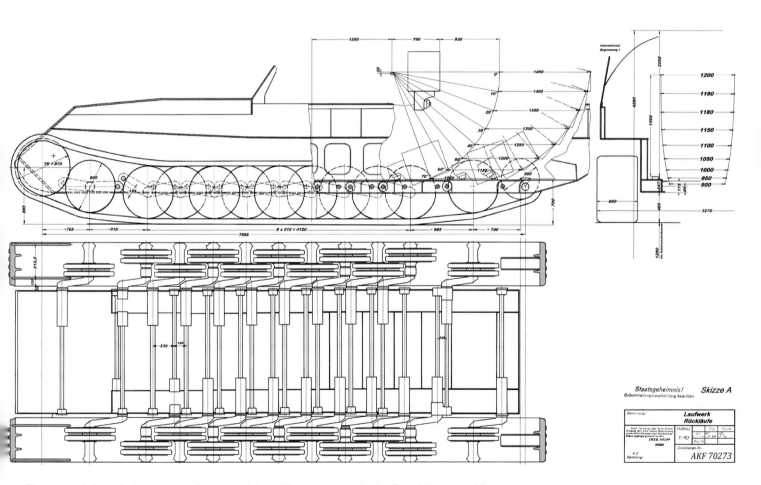

The possible barrel elevations and recoils of the 170 mm cannon in the *Geschützwagen* VI.
Above right, the necessary area for the recoil of the 170 mm barrel traversed 5°.

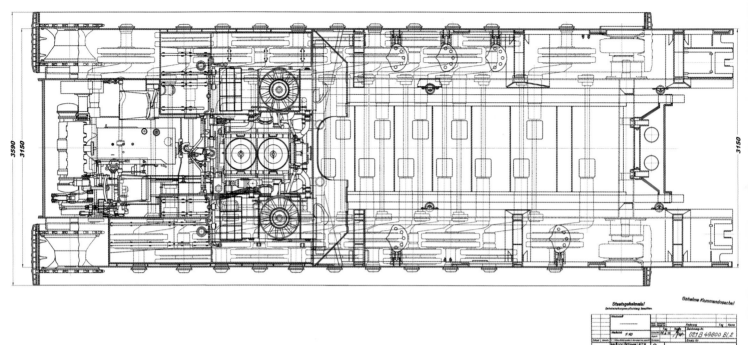

Overhead view of the *Grille* 17 chassis, dated June 29, 1944

On October 31, the Krupp works in Essen were bombed, creating a new problem. Out of concern for the safety of the experimental unit, work was to be completed in another workshop outside; for example, in the Hillersleben area. This also affected the second experimental vehicle, the armored howitzer on the *Panther* gun tank chassis (*s.F.H.* 18/4), also designated *Heuschrecke* 15 by Krupp. The latter had a lengthened *Panther* chassis. With production of the *Panzer IV* coming to an end, the Army Ordnance Office saw the unit as a replacement for the *Hummel* self-propelled gun.

Krupp proposed that assembly should be completed at the Hillersleben firing range with the help of a workshop with experience in assembling the *Tiger*. And so, further work on the *Grille* 17 experimental unit could be continued at Henschel's testing ground near Paderborn with the help of Krupp fitters. This was also fostered by the fact that all necessary workshop facilities, including a crane, were present there. When asked by *Major* Koch of *WuG* 6, Henschel replied that a new shed with a 15-ton crane would be completed at *Panzerstation* 96

Haustenbeck under the direction of *Oberingenieur* Arnoldt at the beginning of 1945.

Thus Krupp's wish for an assembly location for its experimental unit was fulfilled. While the lifting gear at the existing workshop at Haustenbeck was capable of lifting two times 10 tons, it was too unwieldy and would have also significantly interfered with the company's own work. *WuG* 6 and Henschel agreed to meet at the site. Krupp was pleased about this solution, because in addition to the Krupp fitters, experienced *Tiger* people from Henschel would be available for assembly. Krupp also saw this as an advantage for later driving tests with the chassis. *Wa Prüf* 4 considered carrying out the necessary first firing trials at Sennelager, in order to avoid the inevitable transport problems.

With the help of two prime movers belonging to Transport Detachment Speer, on January 1, 1945, the 44-ton tracked vehicle was loaded onto a *Reichsbahn* heavy freight car over an end-loading ramp. On January 4, 1945, Krupp foreman Terwiesche and his fitters drove from Essen to Paderborn.

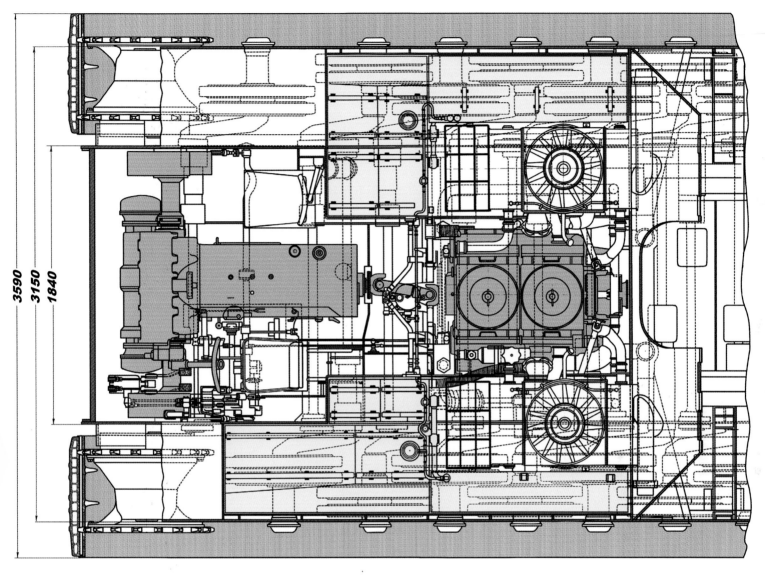

The driver and propulsion compartment of the *Grille* 17/21 in detail. The installed positions of the individual fuel tanks (*yellow*) can be seen to advantage.

A leading engineer from Krupp to oversee the subsequent work had yet to be chosen.

On April 2, 1945, as described in the E-100 chapter, American troops occupied the area around Haustenbeck and with great interest examined all the vehicles there, including the *Grille* 17 experimental unit in the so-called crane hall (10). The running gear finally had the missing road wheel crank arms, though whether tempered or untempered could not be determined. The gun, carriage, and tracks were still missing.

The *Grille* 17 chassis discovered by the Americans in April 1945

The British also towed the *Geschützwagen* VI's chassis from the crane hall in front of the garages (*12*). The vehicle's new owners had previously removed various parts of the internal systems. Evident in this view are the rails on the floor for moving the gun to the rear. There are three seats for the gun crew on the left and right sides. In the upper rear is the hinge for folding the side walls for rail transport.

Seen in front of a *Tiger*, the 170 mm cannon barrel with the so-called "tea strainer" muzzle brake, which weighed approximately 515 lbs. and was 38.8" long.

Behind the *Tiger* seen in the photo above is the *Mörserlafette* 18 (howitzer carriage) and the breech ring of its 170 mm gun.

CHAPTER 4
The Self-Propelled 110-Ton *Räumer S* (Mine-Clearing Vehicle)

The superheavy projects also included another heavyweight from the Krupp company, which developed a self-propelled mine-clearing vehicle designated *Räumer S*. Since the beginning of the Second World War, the Army Ordnance Office had been seeking effective mine-clearing devices to replace the dangerous and time-consuming process of manual mine seeking and removal. In October 1939 the Wegmann company received a contract to develop a so-called hammer blow device to be mounted on the front of the *Panzer* II. The device would set off mines buried in the road before the tank reached them. The commander in chief of the German army felt that the risk to the tank crew was too great, however. Therefore, efforts would also be made to find a safe and practical solution through using remotely controlled mine-clearing vehicles (made of concrete) and towed clearing rollers. Since the mine-clearing vehicle would lead the way and be first to contact the mines, possibly resulting in its destruction, the towed rollers were practically useless.

A mine-clearing version of the *Panzer* III developed the same year seemed to be a more suitable solution. The vehicle was based on a raised *Panzer* III chassis. This offered much-better protection for the crew and the tank chassis, since the shock wave produced by the explosion had time to dissipate. In this case too, towed and pushed mine rollers would be used. The weak spot proved to be the sensitive tracked running gear. On the front of the vehicle there was a pivot for the pushed mine roller.

The concept of two rollers pushed on the track path and a third towed roller could also not be made to work on the heavier *Panzer* IV. The mine rollers, with their relatively small steel discs, were simply too susceptible to damage from exploding mines. After the Army Ordnance Office's not very promising experiments with mine-clearing devices mounted on the front of its tanks, on September 16, 1940, the General Army Office, Inspectorate 5 (Engineer Section), finally issued a contract to the Alkett of Berlin-Borsigwalde and Krupp AG of Essen for the development of a mine-clearing device. Each was to build one prototype, which was to enable the mechanized clearing of mines from roads and open terrain even when fighting was in progress. The vehicle was to be self-propelled

The hammer blow device and the towed mine-clearing rollers during trials in 1940

Minenraumpanzer III, with raised-track running gear

Minenraumpanzer IV, based on the *Panzer* IV with mounted mine-clearing rollers

and, with an attachable roller, was to be capable of clearing a lane 10 ft. wide. The device was not to be greater than 8.85 ft. in height, 10 ft. wide, and 33 ft. long and not weigh more than 44 tons. The vehicle's engine and crew were to be protected against SmK ammunition (rifle bullets with pointed tips and hard metal cores). Each company was to build one prototype for use in operational trials.[22]

The Alkett Design

The two companies followed different paths with their designs. Alkett developed a mine-clearing vehicle with three rollers, weighing approximately 60 tons, whose weight was supposed to set off the mines. Only the two forward rollers were pushed, the rear roller being towed. They were also used to steer the vehicle, which was accomplished mechanically. Powered by a 300 hp Maybach HL-120 engine from the *Panzer* IV, the vehicle was 20.6 ft. long, 10.5 ft. wide, and 9.5 ft. tall. The Alkett designers equipped their vehicle with the machine gun turret from the *Panzer* I. The vehicle's 31.5-inch ground clearance and 0.8 to 1.8 inches of armor were supposed to protect the two-man crew from the exploding mines. Furthermore, inside there was a double floor to protect the drive system. The drive rollers and the rear roller were 25 inches wide. The lanes did not cover the entire vehicle width;

therefore, use of the vehicle with just a towed mine roller could make sense. The effective clearing width was 74.8 inches, with a track width of 125 inches. Thus about 40 percent of the total width could not be covered.

Each roller had a track with a type of shoe developed by Dr. Koppisch of Nuremberg. These were highly reminiscent of the roller drums used by heavy guns from the First World War, which were supposed to prevent the narrow iron wheels from sinking into the ground. The effective ground pressure on level ground was 27 psi, and 18.5 psi with a sink depth of 4 inches. The calculations were based on a weight of just over 42 tons, as determined by Soviet test engineers. Theoretically, the weight of 60 tons specified by the Army Ordnance Office gave a ground pressure with no sink depth of about 48 psi.

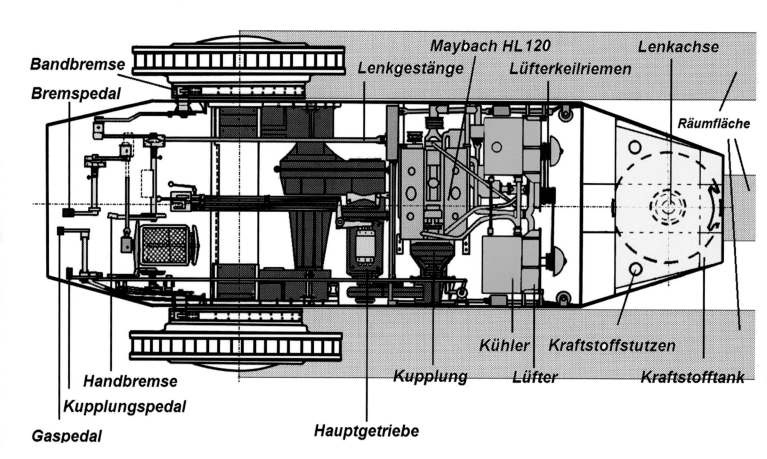

Cross section of the Alkett mine clearer and its assemblies. The vehicle's effective clearing area is also shown to advantage.

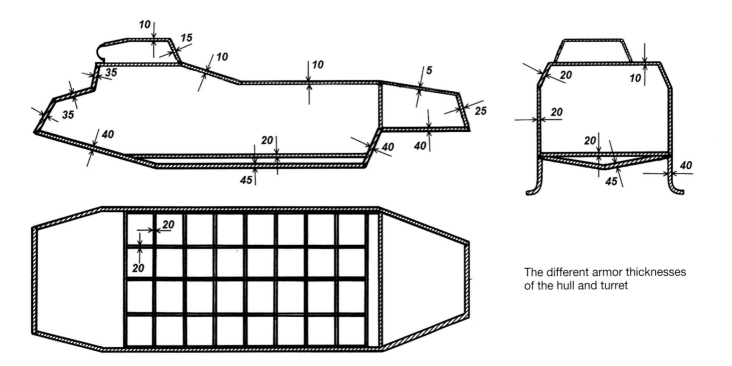

The different armor thicknesses of the hull and turret

The Alkett mine-clearing device in front of the main building of the artillery range at Kummersdorf

The hinged shoes were so designed that two to three plates were in contact with the ground at any time, which thus increased the track contact area. Each plate was about 25 × 20 inches. Damaged elements could be replaced easily. Driving tests on a sandy forest lane at the Kummersdorf firing range in 1943 revealed a maximum speed of 9 to 12 mph. Higher speeds were not possible, since centrifugal force caused the shoes to lift. They also produced a very loud ambient noise. During one of the first test drives the steering mechanism also broke.[23]

Technically the Alkett mine clearer was still far from ideal, but it never had the opportunity to reach maturity since priorities changed: after 1943, the need for German troops to clear mines diminished steadily, given that mines are a defensive weapon whose primary task is to hinder offensive forces. And by that time the Germans were hardly in a position to carry out large offensive actions.

The completed prototype was captured by the Soviets at the Kummersdorf firing range in April 1945 and, in 1946, was taken to Kubinka near Moscow. The Russians tested the device's suitability until July 1947. Since September 1978, the Alkett mine-clearing vehicle has been on display in the Kubinka Tank Museum.

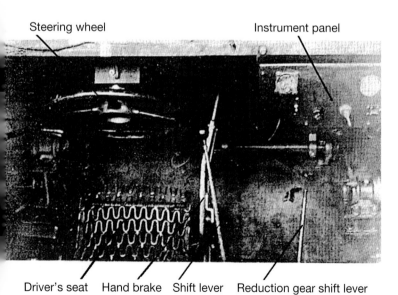

Steering wheel   Instrument panel

Driver's seat   Hand brake   Shift lever   Reduction gear shift lever

The driver's compartment of the Alkett mine clearer and its control elements

The Krupp Design

Krupp took another path with its design. It resembled the later prototype of a heavy recovery vehicle (Lauster Wargel LW 5). The similarities showed in the two identical vehicle parts connected by a Cardan joint-steering system. The oversized wheels gave the vehicle enormous pulling force off-road, and in Krupp's view this was necessary for the *Räumer S* if it was to be able to move and control heavy mine-clearing rollers. Together with the vehicle's large ground clearance, the tall but narrow steel wheels provided better protection against mines compared to tracked vehicles such as the *Minenräumer* III, since tracked running gears were much more susceptible to mine damage.

Krupp therefore designed a two-part vehicle on 9.0 ft. high barrel-like steel wheels. Its dimensions clearly exceeded those in the Army Ordnance Office's specification. The vehicle was 51.25 ft. long, 10.7 ft. wide, and 12.9 ft. tall. Because the large wheels were not steerable, the mine-clearing vehicle had a hydraulic Cardan joint-steering system. Both halves of the vehicle could turn 22 degrees to either side. Two driver's positions, one for forward travel and one for driving backward, were intended to improve maneuverability. The crew consisted of two men. Each half of the vehicle was powered by a Maybach HL 90 P-30 K engine (9-liter displacement, tank engine for 22-ton tanks, with clutch housing). The gasoline engine was a prototype, one of a small series built by Maybach.

The 36-ton prime mover made by Lauster in 1943

Krupp received a total of six engines, which were also used in two other Krupp projects, the *le.Flak* (*VFWL*) and the *Pz.Sfl.IVc*. These engines produced 350 hp at a then unusually high speed of 4,000 rpm. Operating speed was 3,600 rpm, which was sufficient for an output of 330 hp. Since the engine developed its power from revolutions, it needed less displacement, which also resulted in a considerable weight savings: at 1,543 lbs., the engine was relatively light, with the Alkett mine-clearing vehicle having the considerably heavier HL 120 (2,028 lbs.) with a displacement of 12 liters. The downside of this design was the presumed shorter operating life of the high-revving engines.

The Maybach HL 90 twelve-cylinder V engine

Maybach HL 90 P 20 K

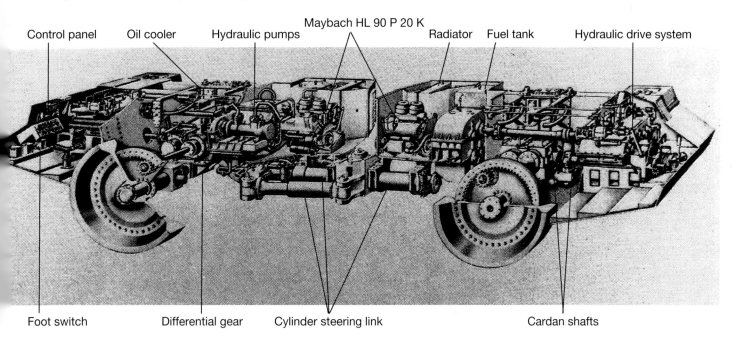

Control panel   Oil cooler   Hydraulic pumps   Radiator   Fuel tank   Hydraulic drive system

Foot switch   Differential gear   Cylinder steering link   Cardan shafts

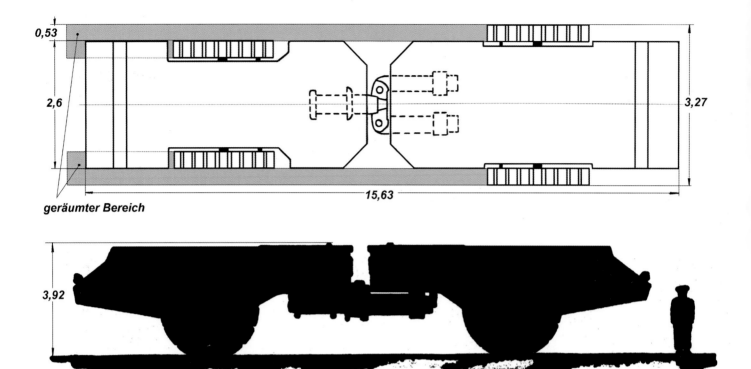

0,53

2,6

3,27

geräumter Bereich

15,63

3,92

The HL 90 forwarded its output both to the Imo hydraulic pumps and the Krupp hydraulic drive systems, which made synchronization of the two engines unnecessary. A blade adjustment in the hydraulic drive systems made it possible to start and regulate speed. These drive systems together with a manual gearbox were located in each driver's position. There was a differential transmission for driving each axle, and liquid brakes would slow the vehicle. Mechanical band brakes functioned as a parking brake. To minimize the explosive effect of detonated mines, in addition to the high ground clearance of 3 to 5 ft., the Krupp designers envisaged that the steel wheels would have a large interleaving capability, which would not only absorb the energy from the explosions but also be able to cross the resulting mine craters. The designers also included sprung single seats for the drivers and machinists as a protective measure for the crew. A *Fahrersehklappe* 50 driver's visor and the KFF 2 driver's lens were envisaged for each driver's position.

Exactly like the Alkett MMB vehicle, the drive wheels could not cover the entire width of the vehicle, although the wheels of the Krupp mine clearer had different gauges. Therefore, complete coverage could be achieved only in combination with a pushed or towed mine-clearing device.

Krupp progressed quickly with construction of the prototype, but like other tank projects, enemy action spoiled all the plans. An indication of this is the draft report from June 11, 1943, on the occasion of a meeting between Krupp-AK and *Wa Prüf* 5/III, which touches on the possibilities of obtaining replacements for destroyed parts. Krupp proposed borrowing two HL 90 P-20K engines from *Wa Prüf* 6/III. After trials with the mine clearer, Maybach would overhaul the engines so that they could be given back to *Wa Prüf* 6/III. A replacement for the two damaged Krupp hydraulic drive systems could not be found, and the equipment and instructions for producing new ones had been destroyed.

Krupp therefore decided to install two Voith hydraulic drive systems. Inquiries to Friedrichshafen revealed that these units should be available for quick delivery. These drive systems did, however, require a redesign of the metal casing, as well as new primary and secondary gear stages. And because the Voith hydraulic drive systems had no blade adjustment, the engine speed and thus vehicle speed could be regulated only by means of newly installed electric actuators. Despite these setbacks, during a subsequent

Assembly of the self-propelled mine clearer in Krupp's second mechanical workshop in Essen. The photo gives a good idea of the proportions of the vehicle, which was more than 49' long.

inspection of the mine clearer while under construction, Krupp was able to convince *Wa Prüf* 5/III of the usefulness of its project. Krupp thus prevented the project from being halted, even though the Alkett vehicle had already completed its initial testing at the Kummersdorf firing range.

Krupp also expressed the desire to complete further assembly "in view of the repeated interruptions" outside Essen. It suggested the company's own firing range at Meppen.[24]

Wa Prüf 5/III agreed in principle and ultimately approved the Pioneer Experimental Site (Site F) at the Hillersleben Testing Station for assembly of the Krupp mine clearer. A workshop hall was founded in the firing range's artillery workshop (Site B). Further assembly work took place there from the end of August 1943, after the Army Ordnance Office had authorized a workshop crane, the provision of support staff, and the supplying of a wide range of materials

and services. *Wa Prüf* 5/III planned the first driving tests with the mine-clearing device on May 16 and 17, 1944. Since the self-propelled mine-clearing device was not operational at that time, a tank was to be used for propulsion. In this context the previously cited report mentions a tank that had sat in the open at the artillery workshop for two years. This suggests that it was the *Minenräumer* III, which was then at Hillersleben. After the two batteries were installed, the coolant was warmed, and rainwater was drained, the coupled mine clearer was easily maneuvered backward on the street. It was only the attachment for the *Räumer S*, however, since the participants did not inspect the self-propelled mine clearer until a day later in the artillery workshop. This was followed by a demonstration of the mine-clearing equipment.

First the tank drove with the roller in front, after the fitters had latched the locking mechanism. On the smooth road, gentle curves were easily negotiated, since the rubber-mounted rollers yielded in their forks. Maximum speed was about 13 mph. On curved roadway, however, the direction had to be constantly corrected, which put a great strain on the tank's brakes. The driving test had to be interrupted several times because the brakes smoked so badly that the driver temporarily had to get out of the vehicle. Since the weight to be guided had roughly doubled compared to the tank, the mine clearer must have weighed about 66 tons. The test finally had to be halted after the tank shed a track; the next day, the track was put back on with the help of six winches. Steering in reverse proved so difficult that a roughly 8-inch-thick oak tree was knocked over. It turned out that steering on soft ground was impossible in this configuration.

Changes in direction could be accomplished only by backing up and starting over. The poor visibility for the driver, caused by the large clearing rollers, meant that the driver had to rely on a guide. Because of its great weight, the possible use of this development was questioned; however, in a report from July 1943, Krupp recognized an advantage in the vehicle's weight: "that the weight of the Krupp vehicle with four powered rollers may be 121 tons [double that of the Alkett vehicle] with no loss in technical performance. It should be borne in mind that the total weight affects the drive rollers and thus the coefficient of friction between the ground and the rollers can be used 100 percent. The weight of the Alkett vehicle is divided between three rollers; therefore only about two-thirds of it can be utilized. Furthermore, the towing of the third roller represents an unfavorable aspect, which is totally absent from ours. Incidentally the Krupp mine clearer has a total weight of only about 82 tons, which means that its driving characteristics should be considerably better."[25]

Consequently, the mine clearer that was to be attached must have weighed about 82 tons. On the other hand, the vehicle had to be heavy to ensure that the mines detonated. At the same time, a suitably heavy towing vehicle had to be available for the mine-clearing equipment. The designers had reinforced the upper nose armor to allow for installation of the mount for the attachment gear. It was not, as might have been suspected, supplementary armor.

The 8.85 ft. steel rollers had tracks with rubber plates about 21 × 27 inches in size. On firm ground just one plate was in direct contact with the ground. Average ground pressure with a vehicle weight of 120 tons was about 170 psi. The device probably could not have been used in the field, since the *Maus* tank's ground pressure of 20.6 psi on firm surfaces was considered barely acceptable and caused severe damage to roads.

The End
of the Krupp Project

On May 18, 1944, there was a meeting and an inspection of the self-propelled mine clearer at Hillersleben. The Army Ordnance Office gave its approval for assembly to continue, especially since the new head of the Testing Group, *Generalleutnant* Schneider, displayed great interest in the project. Meanwhile, the Voith hydraulic drive systems and the Imo pumps (screw spindle pumps) had arrived. After opening the units, the engineers found that one hydraulic drive and one pump were very dirty inside and had to be thoroughly cleaned before installation. At the beginning of June they completed fitting the drives and pumps to the gear train layout, likewise the installation of the electric actuators. On August 9, 1944, there was another inspection by *Wa Prüf* 5/III at Hillersleben. The responsible representatives of the authorities urged that the device be completed by the end of September, and made reference to the British leaflet that showed a mine clearer "that consists of a tank with a rapidly rotating drum in front, crosswise to the direction of travel, and attached chains that flail the ground. The drum is powered by means of a universal shaft and bevel gear mechanism powered by the tank's engine. According to the leaflet, these mine clearers have been used successfully in Africa. Recently it was used with equal success in the invasion zone."[26]

A *Führer* order called for preliminary tests for a similar device. It was pointed out, however, that similar experiments had been conducted years before, which had not been successful. The French had also had no success with a similar mine-clearing device.

Before assembly was completed, the Army Ordnance Office received the final bill for the self-propelled mine clearer. Krupp listed 6,150 designer days, this figure having been inflated by the conversion work made necessary by the bomb damage. On September 15, 1944, *Wa Prüf* 5 advised Krupp by telegram that all work on the mine clearer was to be halted immediately and that the fitters were to be released. Six days later, however, the fitters at Hillersleben received a telegraph from their employer telling them that the mine clearer was to be completed. Then on September 23, an *Oberst* from *Wa Prüf* 5 turned up at Hillersleben and asked about the final completion date, which was to be the beginning of October at the latest. The Army Ordnance Office made available 317 gallons of gasoline and 26 gallons of standard engine oil for the planned testing and inspection.

In the last surviving report, dated October 20, 1944, the leading Krupp fitter at Hillersleben informed his company that the last deadline for completion, October 15, 1944,

This is how the Americans found the vehicle at the Artillery Workshop in Hillersleben in 1945.

could not be met and that the work, though proceeding smoothly, would take until early November. The planned testing of the device could then take place at the Kummersdorf range. The work at Hillersleben was completed in early November, and the fitters set out to return to Essen. Letters from late October 1944 have survived, in which *Wa Prüf* 6/IIIb requested the return of the six Maybach HL 90 P-20 K and HL 90 Le engines it had been loaned as quickly as possible for use in new experimental vehicles. Since all the received letters at Krupp-AK-Grusonwerk Magdeburg burned on August 5, 1944, it was possible to determine the whereabouts of only four of the six engines being sought by December 27, 1944:

■ Engine No. 115001: on April 2, 1943, delivered to Krupp AK–Grusonwerk Magdeburg on behalf of armament agency for the *le.Flak* 4 (*VFWL*) project and installed there

■ Engine No. 115003: sent to Alkett on behalf of *Wa Prüf* 6 on July 30, 1943
■ Engine No. 115005: sent to Maybach-Motorenbau in Wangen/Allgäu on behalf of *Wa Prüf* 6/III on September 21, 1944
■ Engine No. 115006: delivered to Krupp AK–Grusonwerk Magdeburg for *Pz.Sfl.*IVc project on behalf of *Wa Prüf* 6/I on August 5, 1941, and installed

As to the other two HL-90 engines installed in the mine clearer, the affected staff of the Krupp-Grusonwerk apparently had no information. Thus, on the German side, information about the self-propelled mine clearer disappeared. The advancing American troops captured the vehicle at Hillersleben and sent it to the collection center for captured weapons in France for testing. What became of it afterward is unknown.

One segment during transport by rail for testing near Paris. Special support carriages were used to transport one-half of the vehicle. In the process, all trace of the vehicle disappeared.

CHAPTER 5
The Tank Projects of Engineer Edward Grote

Ideas about the ideal size of armored vehicles had not yet reached their climax, however. The designers' imaginations created tracked land battleships, which were more reminiscent of extraterrestrial objects than real tanks. The military imagined parallels to naval warfare on land, where an armored cruiser with countless guns sought to break through a blocking force on the high seas. Whereas a battleship had the open sea on which to maneuver, the question arose, Where should a land ship drive on solid ground?

Apart from deserts and steppes, such large, open surfaces existed only in the far east of Russia. It was therefore logical that the then Soviet Union should make a serious effort to develop such vehicles, especially since Soviet industry was making huge efforts to develop the nation.

First we should turn to the preceding tank designs of the creators of the 1,000-ton tank that later became the Rat. The Soviet Union was then making a major turn toward technology, turning an agrarian country into an industrial one. Of course,

The 77-ton French Char 2C breakthrough tank

this also affected the mechanization of the Red Army. On April 11, 1929, therefore, the Council of People's Commissars of the USSR decided to develop a heavy tank that was to be similar to the French Char 2C breakthrough tank.

Since there were few experienced Soviet tank designers at that time, and because of the limited time available, it was decided to bring in foreign tank designers. Following a visit by a Russian delegation in 1932, even Professor Porsche was invited to spend several weeks in the Soviet Union. Upon his return he showed himself to be deeply impressed by the Soviets' technical achievements: "I never knew that there were such modern factories in Russia."[27]

The Leningrad design bureau AVO-5 in a photograph taken in 1931: in the front row are, *from left to right* (position and nationality in brackets): Nina Chermak (engineer-designer, Russian), Karl Ottersbach (head of the Grote tank design group, German), Edward Grote (chief designer, German), Nikolay Barikov (head of AVO-5, later worked on the T-28, T-35, and T-100; Russian), Sevrugin (engineer, Russian).

In the second row (*from left to right*): Friedrich Hufschmidt (engineer, German), Vladimir Znievsky (designer, Russian), Maxim Somos (engineer, Russian), Pavel Flintsev (engineer, Russian), Boris Zhukov (engineer, Russian), Tamara Fedorova (engineer, Russian), Kinolay Korzunov (engineer, Russian), Besonov (engineer, Russian), Herman Feldhusen (engineer-designer, German).

Karl-Otto Saur, later state secretary in the armaments ministry, visited the Soviet Union on a study trip in 1931. On his return he was impressed by the Soviet central control and its demands for technical advancement.[28]

Defense Minister K. J. Voroshilov and People's Commissar Chalepski personally selected the German design bureau of Edward Grote from three candidates. The reasons given by the commissars were that one of the engineers in Grote's design bureau was a member of the German Communist Party, and Grote himself was sympathetic toward the Soviet Union. In March 1930, therefore, the German engineers were invited to the Soviet Union. On April 5, 1930, Grote received a highly secret contract to initiate a project for a heavy breakthrough tank with the same composition as the T 12 tank or the French twin-turret Char 2C. Its essential characteristics included a weight of 44 tons, a 76 mm cannon or a 122 mm howitzer, a 37 mm antitank gun, five machine guns, and armor more than 0.8 inches thick. For this purpose, design bureau AVO 5, led by Nicolai Barykov, was formed in the Bolsheviki factory in Leningrad.[29]

On April 22, 1930, the engineers selected a model with a long-barreled 76 mm gun with a semiautomatic breech from several design sketches. A 1:10 scale wooden model was built. The project was designated TG after chief designer Grote and was top secret. Technical examination was carried out by the factory's chief designer, Engineer Ginsburg, and Professor Zaslavskov. A preliminary report on the tank by committee member Chalepski to Commissar Voroshilov contained the first technical information:

- a 360-degree rotating turret with a 37 mm antitank gun and muzzle velocity of 3,000 fps
- a 76 mm A19 antiaircraft gun on the floor of the turret
- two machine guns on each side
- another machine gun in the rear of the turret
- The hull was welded for the first time with 1.7 inches of armor in front.
- 0.8 to 0.9 inches on the sides
- 0.4 to 0.6 inches on the hull floor and roof
- vehicle length was approximately 275 inches

The designers had created road wheels with a hollow rubber tire, which was supposed to result in a very smooth ride. The drive sprockets were to have hooks for added traction when crossing ditches or trenches. With these, Edward Grote hoped to achieve a trench-crossing capability of a considerable 16 to 20 ft. The four-speed transmission (forward and reverse) was separate from the air-cooled engine, which produced 250 hp. The planned engine had special lubrication for each cylinder, which was supposed to result in a very smooth-running power plant. Grote envisaged a control stick similar to that of an aircraft as the control element. Pneumatically assisted, the vehicle's steering was very smooth; moving the joystick to the side caused the tank to turn. Driving and braking were accomplished by pushing the stick forward or pulling it back.

The vehicle's suspension consisted of three elements:

- coil springs for all ten large road wheels
- an air spring for each wheel
- the hollow rubber tires

It was thus possible for the tank to drive on roads on the five pairs of large road wheels after the tracks were removed. Grote took this combined running gear from the American Christie suspension, which had previously been used on the BT series of tanks. New to Soviet tank design was the stroboscope-like observer cupolas for the commander and driver. This principle of counterrotating stroposcope cupolas (400 to 500 rpm) had proved itself on the French Char 2 tank. Depending on the type of fuel, the tank's range was to be 185 to 217 miles.

The factory had completed 85 percent of the work on the first vehicle, and it was to be ready for testing by December 1, 1930. When Commissar Voroshilov visited the factory in Leningrad on November 17, he saw the prototype sitting unfinished. In addition, Edward Grote fell seriously ill, further delaying the project. The complicated air-cooled M 6 eight-cylinder engine, in particular, caused problems, and so as a stopgap, in April 1936, the M 6 eight-cylinder liquid-cooled engine had to be fitted to allow testing to begin. The engine came from the previous T-24 tank project. This 300 hp engine

had larger dimensions than the planned air-cooled engine, and the hull had to be reworked to accommodate it. Instead of a four-speed transmission, a servo-assisted six-speed transmission was installed, which enabled the tank to be driven at the same speed forward and backward. The vehicle's weight ultimately rose to 31.4 tons. Range off-road fell to 93 miles.

By July 1931, the vehicle was finally ready for testing, which was supposed to last until October 1, 1931. The vehicle demonstrated satisfactory maneuverability and handled well. A maximum speed of 21 mph was achieved during testing. Power transmission proved very effective, and with its pneumatically assisted controls, the tank was easy to control, the joystick being used to accelerate, brake, and steer the tank. This technology made the design and tuning very complicated. Low-quality rubber collars resulted in problems sealing the compressed air cylinder, and further serious design shortcomings also came to light. The fighting compartment for the crew of five proved extraordinarily cramped, and access to the power train and suspension was severely restricted. The testers also criticized the design of the tracks because of their poor traction.

At the conclusion of testing, on October 4, 1935, the committee, made up of representatives of the Red Army, industry, and the designers of AVO 5, found that while the designers had gained many new and positive insights with the tests, the vehicle was a purely experimental tank with which the engineers could test all mechanisms. Even after its shortcomings had been addressed, production would have been out of the question because of the tank's extremely high cost of more than 1.5 million rubles. For comparison the committee used the production cost of a BT-2 tank of just 60,000 rubles. Nevertheless, on the basis of this "Tank Grote" (TG-1), Edward Grote undertook the design of the "Tank Grote 3" (TG-3). The design for this larger and heavier tank had two parallel engines and transmissions, each of which was to power one track.

The crew consisted of seven men. Grote presented this design to the tank committee on December 3, 1931. While it acknowledged the designer's inventiveness and imagination, it found that he had no experience in tank design. Compared to the TG-1, the design was too cumbersome and even more complicated. Despite this, in May 1932, Grote presented the design for an even-heavier tank, the "Tank Grote 6" (TG-6c), which Grote developed into the T-42 breakthrough tank one

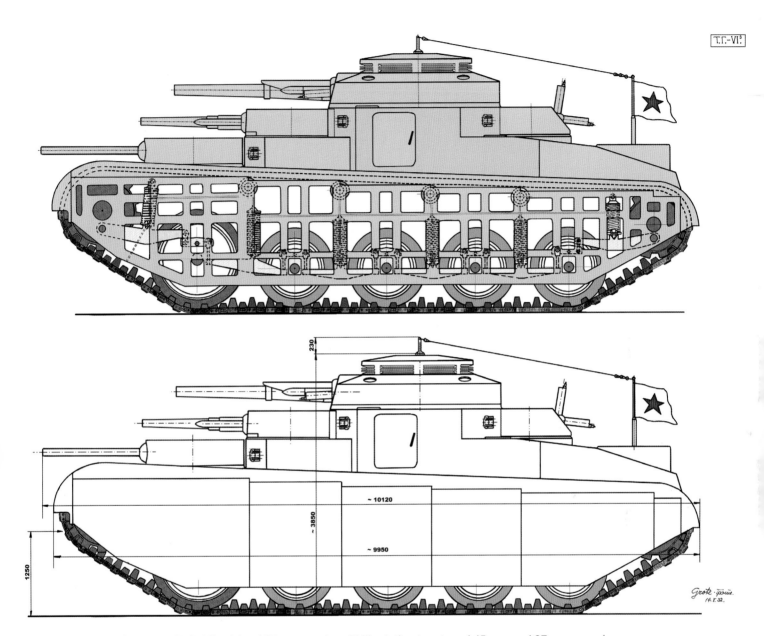

Design of a "Tank Grote" 6c (T.G.-VI), with a 107 mm gun in a 360° rotating turret, and 45 mm and 37 mm guns (one each) in partly rotating turrets. In the rear were two more turrets with twin machine guns for antiaircraft defense.

year later. This design had a 76 mm gun turret forward, and behind the large 107 mm gun turret there was also a 45 mm gun turret. The tank had a simplified suspension. The 1,600 hp sixteen-cylinder engine was supposed to be an in-house development and enable a speed of 22 mph.

The Soviet leadership lost interest in Edward Grote's imaginative designs, however. Because of his expensive and complicated tanks and the trend toward heavy medium tanks, the Soviets had no further need of the German engineers. At that time, the beginning of the 1930s, the Soviet

The British A1E1 Independent multiturret tank, the inspiration for the Soviet T-35

designers oriented themselves on the British A1E1 Independent multiturret tank and the Mark III, a developed version, a land warship-type vehicle from a known producer, to develop a heavy breakthrough tank.

The Soviet engineers focused on an uncomplicated structure, simplicity of operation, and the problem-free production of large numbers, since the Red Army had few qualified men and mechanics to maintain and service these vehicles. This development led Edward Grote's former employer, the Bolshevik Factory in Leningrad, to develop the heavy, multiturret T-35 tank in 1933, which alongside the T-28 ultimately led tank development at that time into a dead end. But Germany also dedicated herself to the trend with the *Großtraktor* and the *Neubaufahrzeug* projects. In the US, the 61-ton M-6 heavy multiturret tank project appeared in 1940.

In March 1933, despite the Red Army's disinterest in his designs, Grote presented designs to War Commissar Tukhachevsky in the form of etchings of a 1,000-ton (1,100 metric ton) so-called fortress tank. It is very likely that there never was an official written contract. The letter illustrated

The British Mark III multiturret tank, the inspiration for the Soviet T-28

The Soviet T-35 multiturret tank, which was inspired by British designs with multiple turrets

Built in the 1930s, the German *Neubaufahrzeug* multiturret tank

The American M-6 multiturret tank, with one 76.2 mm and one 37 mm gun plus five or six machine guns.

Moskau, den 4.März 1933.
1.Koptelski Per.9 - 123.

Am

Marschall Duchatschewski,

Kriegsministerium,

M o s k a u.

Sehr verehrter Genosse Duchatschewski,

in der Annahme, dass Sie sich meiner Arbeiten in Leningrad, sowie der konstruktiven Vorschläge zum schweren Durchbruchtank erinnern, bitte ich mir zu gestatten, Ihnen zwei Radierungen des Projekts des grossen Festungstanks (1000 Tonnen) zu zusenden in der Erwartung, Ihre wohlwollende Aufmerksamkeit auf dieses moderne Verteidigungsmittel zum Schutz der UdSSR zu lenken. Die Konstruktion ist vollkommen durchgereift und sehr gut möglich und wohl wertvoll in Anbetracht der politischen Weltspannungen und des Krieges im Osten.

Leider haben sich für mich die persönlichen Verhältnisse seit meinem einjährigen Aufenthalt in Moskau nicht günstig entwickelt. Die sich meinen Plänen entgegenstellenden Schwierigkeiten lassen mich keine Möglichkeit erkennen in der Zukunft meine Energien auch nur zu einem Teil entfalten zu können.

Ich wäre Ihnen dankbar für eine persönliche Aussprache, so wie Sie solche mir früher im Leningrad gewährten.

Mit Hochachtung,

ergebenst

Edward Grote.

E.Grote, O.K.G. Spezmaschtrest.

112

Designed to function as
a mobile bunker, this
tank was supposed to
defend the nation
against attacks from
the sea. The borders of
the Soviet Union were
too extensive for them
to be guarded by
massive bunker
installations like those
of the Maginot Line.

here also touches on the problems that Grote had in the Soviet Union at that time. He must have taken ownership of this development direction, which was later reflected in the zeal for his later 1,000-ton projects.

The key technical data for Grote's "fortress tank" design:

- weight, 1,100 metric tons
- length, 1,338 inches; height, 433 inches; width, 393 inches
- crew of 40
- power provided by twelve supercharged sixteen-cylinder diesel engines of German design, each producing 2,000 hp and resulting in a maximum performance of 17,630 kWH (24,000 hp)
- hydraulic power transmission
- maximum speed of 37 mph
- climbing ability of 189 inches
- wading depth of 315 inches
- Track contact area of 20,000 mm produced a theoretical ground pressure of 10.25 psi.
- On each side of the tank there were three tracks, each 39 inches wide.

Armor consisted of
- forward and turret armor (11.8 inches),
- side armor (9.8 inches),
- roof armor (3.9 inches), and
- floor armor (2.35 inches).

Armament consisted of
- one turret with two 305 mm guns, 360° of traverse;
- two turrets each with two 152 mm guns, 200° of traverse;
- two turrets each with two 76 mm guns, 200° of traverse; and
- two turrets each with one 45 mm gun, 120° of traverse.

Machine guns were not envisaged because of the tank's concept of operations.

Tukhachevsky passed Grote's documents on to the chairmen of the Military Academy for Mechanization and Motorization (BAMM). The experts there agreed that this design was much too bulky and too complicated. They also predicted considerable problems in the technical design. In

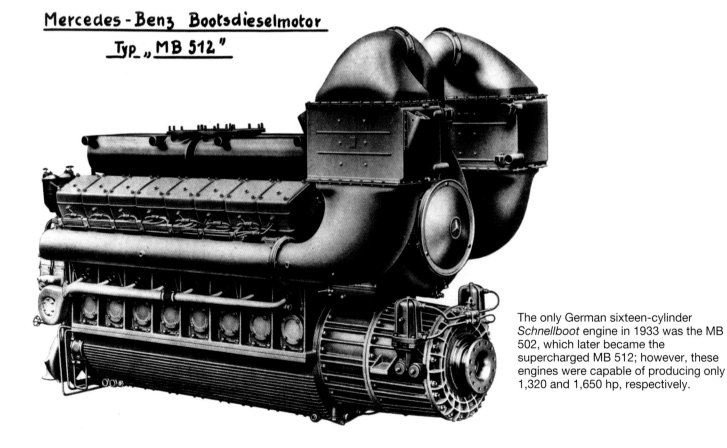

Mercedes-Benz Bootsdieselmotor
Typ „MB 512"

The only German sixteen-cylinder *Schnellboot* engine in 1933 was the MB 502, which later became the supercharged MB 512; however, these engines were capable of producing only 1,320 and 1,650 hp, respectively.

Перспектива художественно оформлена по указаниям и при консультации автора настоящего предложения науч. работ. доцента НИИ инженера Ф.С. Селезнева, — науч. работ. НИИ художн. Н.А. Тусовым.

Проектировал: 16.IV.40г.   рис. № 2.

Soviet design for a land cruiser of April 16, 1940.
The middle tracks would have made steering the vehicle very difficult.

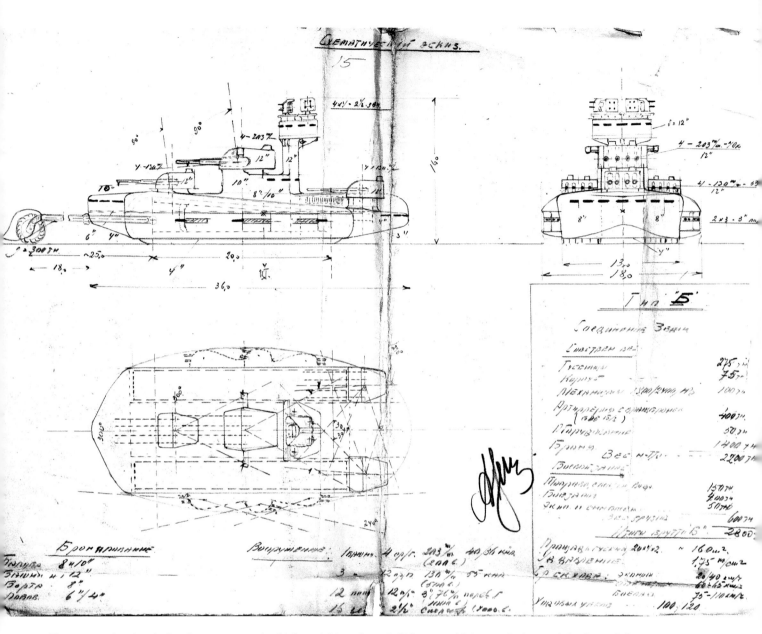

There was also the design for an armored vehicle weighing about 3,086 tons, which was designated the "type B."
The vehicle carried an armament that would have done any battleship proud:

- one turret with four 203 mm guns
- three turrets each with four 130 mm guns
- six 76 mm guns in each side bay

The ship-like conning tower had four quadruple antiaircraft guns for air defense. The height of this "land warship" was 52.5 feet, and it was 59 feet wide and 118 feet long (without the planned mine roller). With its 13-foot-wide tracks, the 65.6-foot track contact area resulted in the enormous ground pressure of 24.9 lbs./in.^{2}. Armor thicknesses were 11.8 inches in the turrets and hull front, while the hull side armor was 7.9 to 9.8 inches thick.

116

the committee's opinion, achieving the planned 24,000 hp engine performance and a speed of 37 mph with a 1,100-metric-ton vehicle would scarcely be possible. But Grote was not alone with his thought processes. Other Soviet designers picked up this theme at that time and designed various "land battleships" in more or less utopian size ranges.

In February 1942, after the Red Army had won the Battle of Moscow, interest in these gigantic projects had still not been extinguished. A breakthrough tank was sought for use against heavily fortified German positions. A detailed design for a 275-ton armored cruiser was developed, which was composed of individual modules from existing tanks such as the heavy KV and T-34. Broken down into individual modules, the tank could more easily be transported by rail and assembled at its destination with the help of quick couplings.

The designers envisaged the tank's armament as a central turret with two 152.4 mm type 1938/40 cannon-howitzers, four 76.2 mm type L-11 of F-34 guns in individual turrets, a retractable type M 1938 76.2 mm antiaircraft gun, two 23 mm automatic cannon (surely the 25 mm M 1940 automatic cannon), three Beresin UBT 12.7 mm machine guns, and fourteen type DT machine guns. Four coupled M-30 or M-40 diesel engines were to produce 4,000 to 6,000 hp. This output was supposed to enable speeds of up to 25 mph. The crew of thirty-four had to be capable of assembling the seven mobile tank segments in thirty hours by using quick couplings and to achieve combat readiness.

On October 6, 1942, the Tank Administration (BTU) advised the development collective that while this design was a success, the wrong path had been chosen for the design of a breakthrough tank, since the normal dimensions and weights of heavy tanks were not to be exceeded. Production of this type would also hinder tank production in general.

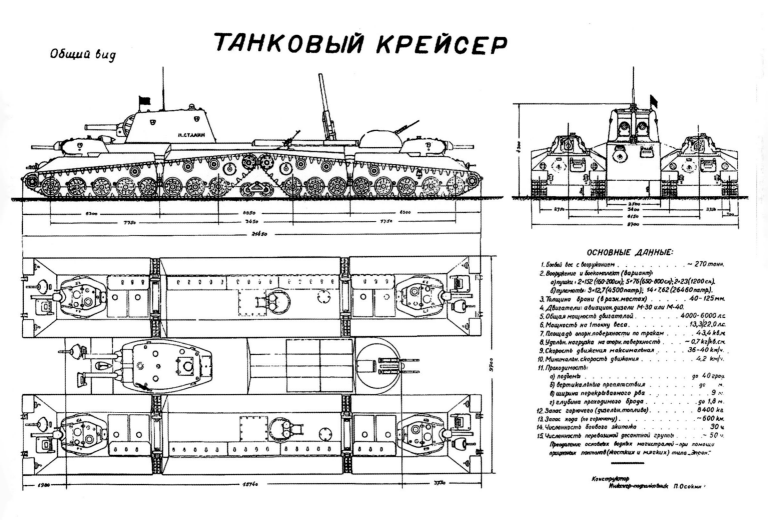

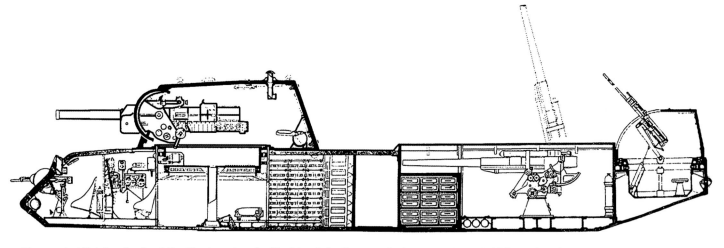

The central fighting body of the "tank cruiser," with driver's/radio operator's compartment, 152 mm howitzer turret, and fighting and ammunition compartments with elevator and antiaircraft positions.

In December 1936, an extensive report on a 1,100-ton tank that a German mechanical engineer had developed in the Soviet Union in the period from 1930 to 1934 appeared in a German weekly magazine unknown to the author. The tank in question was in fact Edward Grote's project for a "1,000-ton fortress tank."

Then, in 1937, an article appeared in the military magazine *Die Kraftfakrkampftruppe*. In it, the Austrian designer and tank specialist G. Burstyn took a position on the report. In summing up, he stated that this design not only was impracticable but was also tactically inexpedient. *Diplom-Ingenieur* Grote was given an opportunity to defend his design. One had to admit that in part Grote was right; many of G. Burstyn's views were outdated. An example of this was Burstyn's claim that a tracked vehicle had to have a ground pressure of no more than 4.7 psi to avoid sinking. This was outmoded thinking, since in 1942 the *Panzer V Panther* tank had good cross-country mobility with a ground pressure of 12 psi. This is to say nothing of the truly high ground pressure of the later E-100 or *Maus* tanks (20.6 psi) or the previously mentioned Soviet project, the type B (25 psi).

A second example of Burstyn's misjudgment was the opinion that a vehicle's maximum speed was dependent on vehicle weight. He assumed that if a light tank was capable of 30 mph and the 77- to 90-ton French Char 2 could manage only 8 mph, then a heavier tank must be even slower. In addition to the necessary engine performance, however, speed was dependent on the suspension and the steering system of the tank in question. The figure of 32 mph for a 1,100-ton tank was of course unrealistic, because at that speed the driving influences on the huge vehicle would not have been controllable.

Grote next presented his lighter tank designs:

■ the TG I, designated T 22 by Grote
■ the TG III, designated T 29 by Grote
■ the TG V, designated T 42 by Grote

Grote's designations did not fit into the Red Army's designation scheme, however, and it has been impossible to verify whether other designations are valid. Soviet reports are also in part contradicted by his accounts, in which he claimed that prototypes of all three were built and had even been tested at Leningrad. It can be proved, however, only that Soviet engineers built and tested the "Tank Grote I." The

alleged demands of Deputy War Commissar Tukhachevsky led to the actual design, with the drawings showing only Grote's first thought processes. The tank's key technical points were as follows:

■ length: 1,338 inches
■ width: 393 inches
■ height: 433 inches
■ fording ability: 315 inches
■ track contact surface: 787 inches
■ track width: 118 inches (39.4 inches per individual track)
■ ground pressure: 11.35 psi
■ ground clearance: 79 inches
■ road wheel diameter: 79 inches
■ armament: two 305 mm guns, four 150 mm guns, and smaller-caliber weapons
■ armor: front, 11.8 inches; sides, 9.8 inches; bottom, 3.9 inches; top, 3 inches
■ propulsion: twelve sixteen-cylinder engines each producing 2,000 hp (there were no sixteen-cylinder diesel engines capable of such performance at that time) as group propulsion systems of six engines each connected via gearing to a left and right main and reduction shaft
■ selective power transmission by means of a hydraulic torque converter or electric transmission
■ wheel mounting by means of hydraulic cylinders with load balancing

This article surely achieved such attention in Germany that German readers could not escape it. Edward Grote, meanwhile, had been named director and installed as special representative for submarine construction attached to the Reich minister for armaments and munitions in the ministry of the same name. At an armaments conference on June 23, 1942, in Berlin, attended by Hitler, Grote spoke about the large tank he had proposed in the Soviet Union. Hitler showed great interest and agreed that the roughly 1,100-ton tank should be determined in sketch form. Grote was to produce a design sketch with Dr. Oskar Hacker, chief designer at Steyr-Daimler-Puch AG and the deputy chairman of the tank development committee. Whether Dr. Hacker was ever actively involved with this theme cannot be verified from the surviving records.[31]

The previously shown drawings represent the first design for a 1,100-ton tank, as requested—according to Edward Grote—by Commissar Tukhachevsky and his defense council.[30]

On July 17, 1942, Director Professor Dr. Müller of Friedrich Krupp AG received a letter from the Armaments Ministry written by *Diplom-Ingenieur* Grote. In it, Grote related that he had received instructions from Hitler via Speer to develop a large tracked vehicle weighing several hundred tons, with 16,000 hp of drive propulsion. He wished to consult with large-transmission specialists from Krupp, especially since the navy high command had told him that Krupp was working on an artillery carrier project on the West Coast and that this project was already at an advanced stage. Grote was referring to the R-2 tracked vehicle mentioned in the previous chapter.

The first meeting between Edward Grote and Dr. Müller took place in Berlin on August 13, 1942, during which Grote presented his first design for a superheavy tank weighing about 88 tons. Its dimensions were 1,375 inches in length

and 550 inches in width. Grote envisaged that the vehicle would be propelled by two large tracked systems, each with three tracks. Each track was to be 47 inches wide. With a track contact area of 827 inches, ground pressure was calculated to be 7.7 psi. For the propulsion system, consideration was being given either to two MAN V 12 Z 32/44 twenty-four-cylinder, double-acting, two-cycle diesel engines, each capable of 8,500 hp at 600 rpm (in reality 10,000 hp rated output at 564 rpm), or eight *Schnellboot* engines by Daimler-Benz, each producing a maximum of 2,000 hp at 1,650 rpm. Grote favored the latter engine, since the eight Daimler-Benz engines, weighing 37.5 tons, were considerably lighter than the two 140-ton MAN engines.

Steering was to be accomplished by speed management of the two tracked systems with the help of a hydraulic Pittler-

The MAN V12Z 32/44, a twenty-four-cylinder, two-stroke, opposed-piston diesel engine, was envisaged for *Kriegsmarine* destroyers.

The twenty-cylinder MB 501 *Schnellboot* diesel engine produced a maximum of 2,000 hp.

Thomas transmission. Two driving ranges were supposed to enable speeds of 1.9 to 7.5 mph and 6 to 25 mph. Grote was unable to give any information concerning armament, the development of this being left to Krupp. The only thing he had was a Krupp drawing of a 305 mm coastal revolving turret (*Kst.Drh.*). He requested twenty designers from Krupp for further work on the project. This was unacceptable to Dr. Müller, who wanted the company to be general contractor. They agreed that Grote should send further designs. On September 18, 1942, Grote wrote to Dr. Müller that he had received documentation from Daimler-Benz AG and MAN-Renk AG for the engines being considered for the project and was therefore able to complete an initial design.

As the next step, Grote urgently required from Krupp information about the mounting and installation of the guns,

since Minister Speer urgently wished to see the first design. The next meeting took place in the armaments representation in Berlin on October 24, 1942, where Grote presented the first designs for discussion. Both spoke about the possible armament, with Dr. Müller proposing a roughly 280 mm main gun, two 128 mm and two 105 mm turrets, and an adequate machine gun armament. Grote promised that he would soon send his designs, and asked that armament proposals be worked out as quickly as possible, which Dr. Müller assured he would do.

On October 10, 1942, Edward Grote sent Dr. Müller a reworked design in which Grote designated the planned large tank as the Project P-1000. He hoped that Krupp specialists would review the projected armament. At that time, Grote had as additional documents those concerning a 280 mm turret gun, the 128 mm antiaircraft gun, and the 88 mm U-boat gun, which he had received from the navy high command. Grote planned the 20 mm *Maschinengewenr* 151 in a rotating mount as the tank's light weapon, this having been recommended by the air force. The most striking difference from his earlier projects was Engineer Grote's emphasis on sloped surfaces and extremely light construction, which were heavily influenced by suggestions from the Air Ministry. He asked that Krupp inform him of its ideas concerning armament, the weight restrictions, and armoring of the turrets, because he was supposed to present his first designs to Speer on October

17. The approximate weight distribution of the individual components was as follows:

- guns: 330 tons
- armor: 220 tons
- framework: 220 tons
- tracks: 110 tons
- engines-transmissions: 110 tons

The resulting total weight of 990 tons caused ground pressure to rise to 9 psi.

Model photo of the first variant of the P-1000 with navy-type twin turrets. Note the large road wheels, which must have had a diameter of at least 98 inches.

Ten days later, on October 20, Grote sent a longitudinal section to Dr. Müller that featured a twin 280 mm gun turret from the *Kriegsmarine*. He saw no problem regarding size, but the weights including ammunition were far too high. Furthermore, he had attempted to install a 128 mm antiaircraft gun on the rear part of the vehicle instead of the 88 mm

U-boat gun. Krupp asked for another meeting with Krupp at its earliest convenience.

Grote's first P-1000 design was largely based on the fortress tank of 1933, with large road wheels and vertical sides. The turrets, taken from warship designs, such as superimposed 280 mm and 128 mm gun turrets, were

characteristic of this first design. Typical of the large naval gun turrets were their bulged sides for the 105 mm rangefinder. The vehicle model also had eight small turrets with the preferred 20 mm MG 151.

On October 31, 1942, Dr. Müller received two more longitudinal views plus a rear view, a front view, a top view, and a longitudinal section of the P-1000. There was obviously no immediate reaction from Krupp, however, since on November 10, Grote requested a response and threatened *Führer* deadlines, but by that time Krupp already had other plans.

When another meeting between Edward Grote and Dr. Müller finally took place on December 17, 1942, Grote presented photos of a new model of the P-1000, but he was then forced to learn that Minister Speer no longer wanted to pursue the project.

Dr. Müller mentioned that Krupp had been given a similar project by Speer; however, he also stated that the Krupp tank had a very different tactical role and that his preparatory work could not be used for it. Edward Grote was told nothing further, however. Dr. Müller stated that behind this tactical role was the design of a superheavy armored howitzer, on which Krupp had been working since the end of the year. The documents do not reveal, however, the extent to which Grote's preliminary work could have been used. The later

Grote design mentioned in the last Krupp documents depicted the P-1000 with harmonically integrated gun turrets.

Grote had reduced the 128 mm flak turrets to two in the forward area, probably for weight reasons, with reduced barrel lengths. With the new lower turrets, he also avoided shot traps. He had reduced the size of the road wheels and thus lowered the unsprung weight. These improvements did not make the project more sensible, however. Grote and the figments of his imagination ultimately failed, especially since his information on weight given in the original documents left much to be desired in terms of believability. Edward F. Grote's trail disappeared after the war in Johannesburg, South Africa, from where he applied for a patent in East Germany on April 28, 1950.

On the following pages are photographs of the later design with organically arranged turrets. As a result of the

The soldier provides a good indication of the size proportions. The ground clearance of 78.75 inches would have allowed a *Panzer* I, with its height of 67 inches, to drive through between the huge vehicle's tracks.

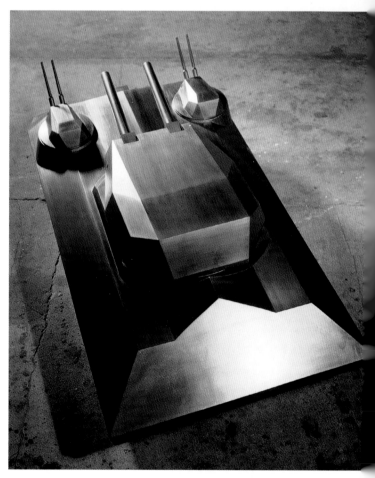

In these photos, the sloped armor plates, which were stressed for the side plates of the third variant and increased the vehicle's width, can be seen to advantage. On the third version shown below, Grote had installed six 20 mm MG 151 cannon on each side and further sloped the tank's armor. This would have once again increased production costs and the total weight of the vehicle.

To better illustrate the size differences, a direct comparison between the P-1000 *Großkampfwagen* and the *Maus* tank

deletion of two smaller turrets and the shortening of the 128 mm guns, the vehicle's weight may have been less than the 800 tons of the first designs. The short-barreled 280 mm guns that were used suggest that Grote received documents from the navy concerning only the obsolete 280 mm L/40 or L/45 rapid-firing cannon. The previously offered 305 mm gun could only have been the obsolete 305 mm gun on the C 1912 L/50 rotating carriage as used on the elderly battleship *Schleswig-Holstein*.

A meeting held on May 14, 1943, showed that Hitler had still not lost interest in the subject of large tanks. By this date a number of other projects had been shown to Hitler at *Führer* headquarters in Rastenburg, including the 1:1 wooden scale model of the *Maus* tank with two flamethrowers and a remotely controlled model of this tank in approximately 1:15 scale. Armaments Minister Speer wrote in his diaries: "At that time the full-size 1:1 scale model of a 180-ton tank that he [Hitler] himself had requested was demonstrated. No one from the tank arm showed any interest in production of this monstrosity, each of which would have cost the capacity for construction of six to seven *Tiger* tanks and would also have created impossible supply and spare-parts problems, was much too

heavy and much too slow [20 km per hour] and moreover could not have been built until 1944. We, meaning Professor Porsche, Guderian, and Zeitzler, had therefore from the beginning agreed to at least express our skepticism through extreme reservation. When Hitler asked him what he thought of the vehicle, Porsche concisely and aloofly said: 'Of course, my *Führer*, we can build such tanks.' The rest of us stood silently in a circle. When Otto Saur [state secretary in the Armaments Ministry, and Speer's deputy] subsequently noted Hitler's disappointment, he began an enthusiastic Suadela about the chances and the technological significance of this monster. . . . Unconfirmed reports that the Russians were building superheavy tanks furthered the exuberance, and in the end, both, free of all technical obstructions, praised the overwhelming fighting power of a tank weighing 1,500 tons, which was supposed to be transported in parts on trains and assembled before going into action. When a highly decorated *Oberst* of the *Panzer* arm finally interjected that a single hand grenade or a Molotov cocktail could set alight this vehicle's oil vapors if it were set off near the cooling air intake, Hitler replied angrily about this annoying comment: 'Then we will just equip this tank with automatic internally

Hitler and those who helped him in the development of these superheavy tank projects. On the right of the photo is *Hauptamtsleiter* Karl-Otto Saur of the armaments ministry, and on the left are the designers of these machines, Director Professor Dr. Erich Müller of Krupp and Professor Dr. Ferdinand Porsche. Between Hitler and Saur, in the black panzer uniform, is *Oberst* Holzhäuer, head of department *Wa Prüf 6*.

These modern drawings are based on the 280 mm C.34 rapid-loading cannon on the C.28 turntable carriage used on the *Gneisenau*.

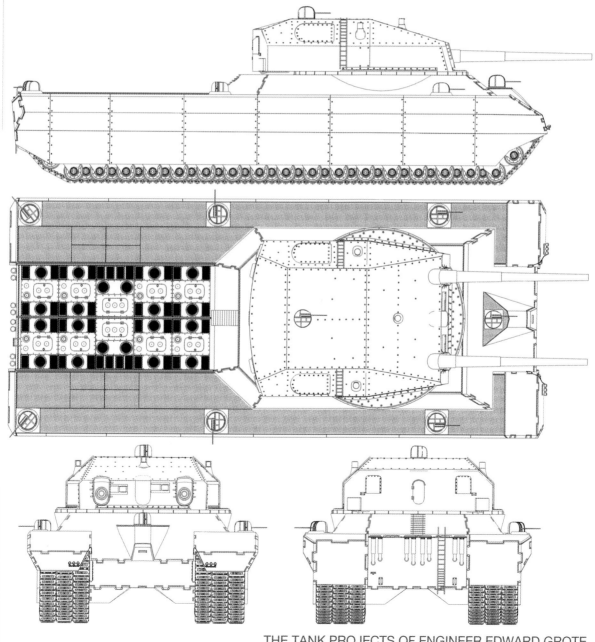

guided machine guns in all directions.' Turning to the *Panzer* colonel, he added in a schoolmasterly tone: 'After all, in all modesty I can claim that I am no dilettante in this field, for I armed Germany.'"[32] This requires no further comment.

This modern sketch is a very speculative representation of the 1,100-ton tank. The original turret from the *Gneisenau* used here has three 280 mm L/54.5 guns. The center 280 mm gun, the 105 mm rangefinder, and the 128 mm antiaircraft gun are missing from these drawings. The internal diameter of the original turret was 401 inches, with 108 inches of separation between guns. The revolving part of the original turret weighed 825 tons (a single gun weighed 58 tons). According to weight distribution, Edward Grote planned 330 tons for all of the guns, which means that the complete *Gneisenau* turret could not possibly have been used, even if one gun was removed and ammunition capacity had been reduced. According to the documents, it was not definitely the turret from the battleship *Gneisenau*, since the *Kriegsmarine* could also have offered Edward Grote a 280 mm SK L/52 C 28 in a three-gun turret from the *Deutschland*-class battleship. There is more information on the 280 mm SK C 34 gun turret from the *Gneisenau*'s Drh.L. 28.

The crew of a turret of the later Oerlandet battery consisted of ten officers and 107 men; therefore, Edward Grote's first concept of a crew of forty per vehicle would have been completely inadequate.

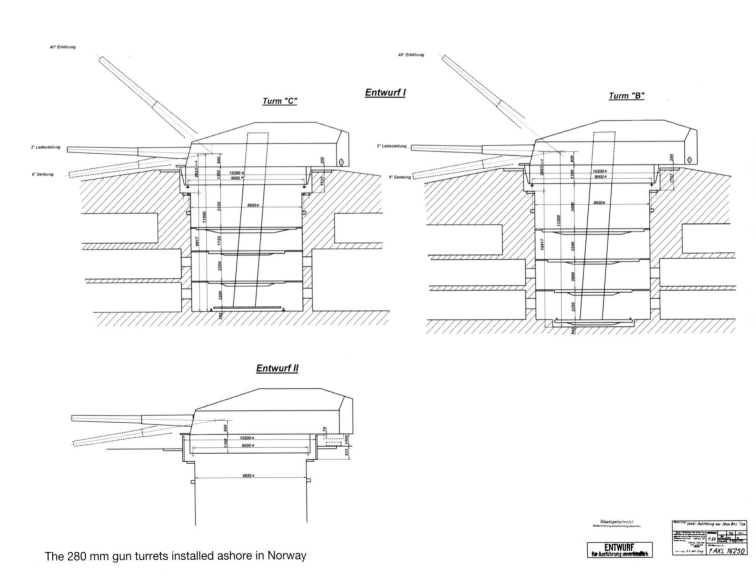

The 280 mm gun turrets installed ashore in Norway

The surviving 280 mm turret C from the *Gneisenau*, formerly the Oerlandet Battery in Norway.

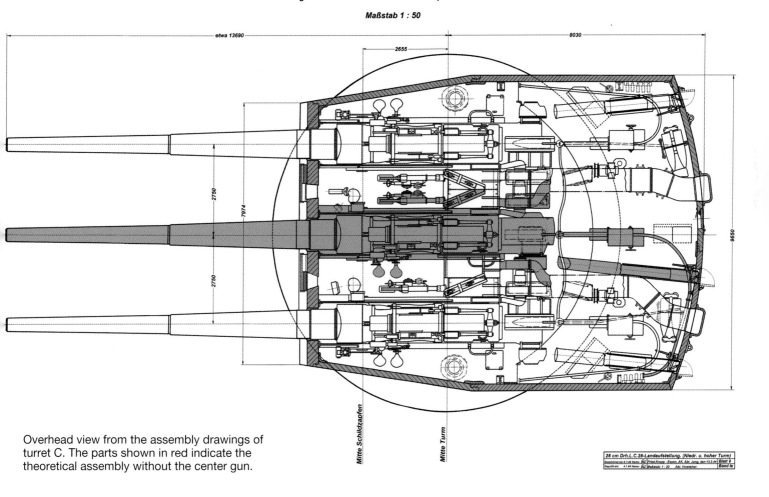

28 cm S.K.C.34 in Drh.L.28 - Landaufstellung.
Waagerechter Schnitt über der Geschützplattform.

Maßstab 1 : 50

Overhead view from the assembly drawings of
turret C. The parts shown in red indicate the
theoretical assembly without the center gun.

Schußrichtung.

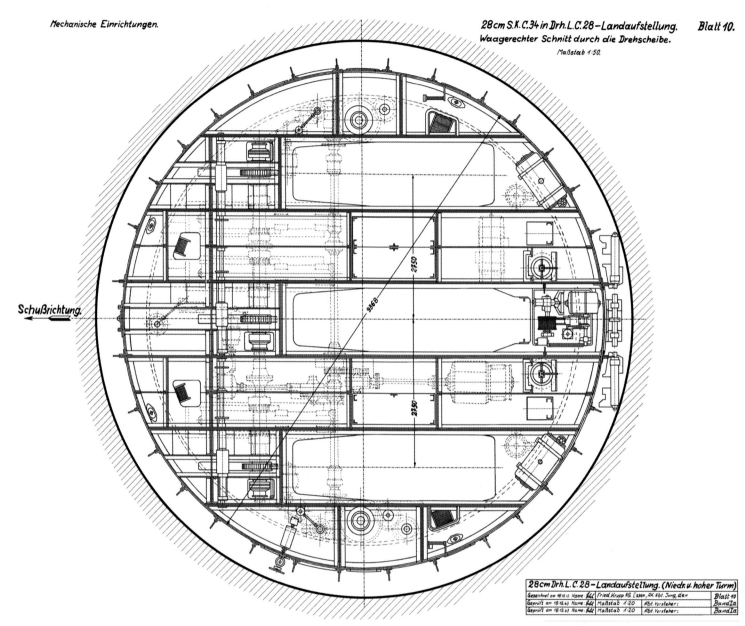

28cm Drh.L.C.28-Landaufstellung. (Niedr. u. hoher Turm)			
Gezeichnet am 18.12.43 Name:	Fried. Krupp AG. Essen, AK. Abt. Jung, den		Blatt 10
Geprüft am 18.12.43 Name:	Maßstab 1:20	Abt. Vorsteher:	Band Ia
Geprüft am 18.12.43 Name:	Maßstab 1:20	Abt. Vorsteher:	Band Ia

The turntable with the necessary elevation and traverse mechanisms for the above turret

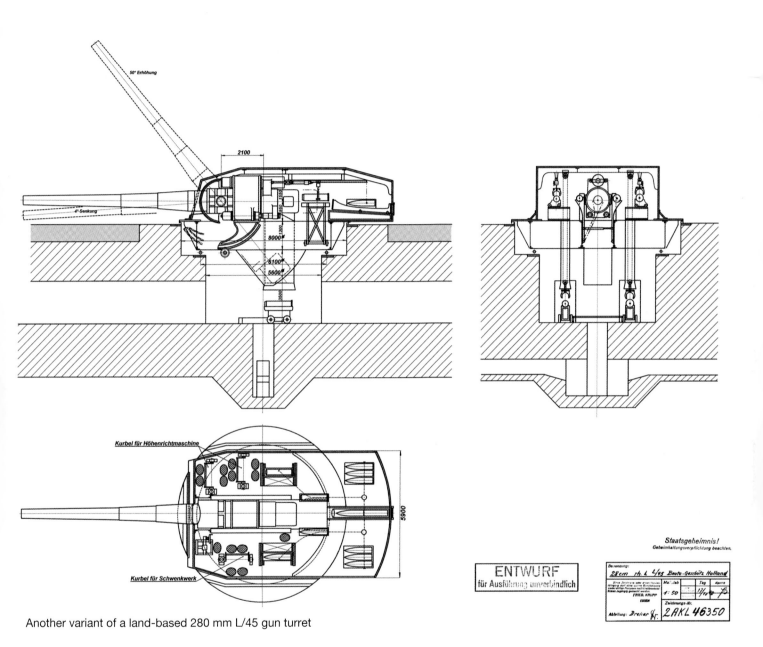

50° Erhöhung

2100

4° Senkung

8000

6100
5600

3600

Kurbel für Höhenrichtmaschine

5900

Kurbel für Schwenkwerk

Another variant of a land-based 280 mm L/45 gun turret

ENTWURF
für Ausführung unverbindlich

Staatsgeheimnis!
Geheimhaltungsverpflichtung beachten.

28 cm rh L ⁴/₄₅ Beute-Geschütz Holland
FRIED. KRUPP
ESSEN
1 : 50
Abteilung: Dreher
2 AKL 46350

From the 120-Ton *Bär* Heavy Howitzer to the 1,000-Ton *Urling* Armored Howitzer

Before going into a discussion of this gigantic project, a previous project must be mentioned: developed by Krupp on its own initiative, so to speak, it was the design for a 305 mm self-propelled gun. First mention of this design took place in March 1943. On March 11, 1943, Dr. Müller presented a design (designation SKA 758) for a heavy self-propelled carriage with a 305 mm L/16 heavy howitzer to the responsible officer of *Wa Prüf* 4/II (artillery department for fortress and combat vehicle artillery). The project's code name was *Bär*

(Bear). At the meeting, Krupp qualified that the designation "assault gun" was not applicable to this vehicle. The firing range of 8 miles given in the design also had to be seen as wrong, since the practical range of the *Mörser* (howitzer) was 6.2 miles. The specification specified that the power train would consist of the Maybach HL 230 engine and the L 801 double-radius steering control of the *Tiger* tank and the ZF-AK7-200 seven-speed transmission of the *Panther* tank. The running gear consisted of interleaved road wheels

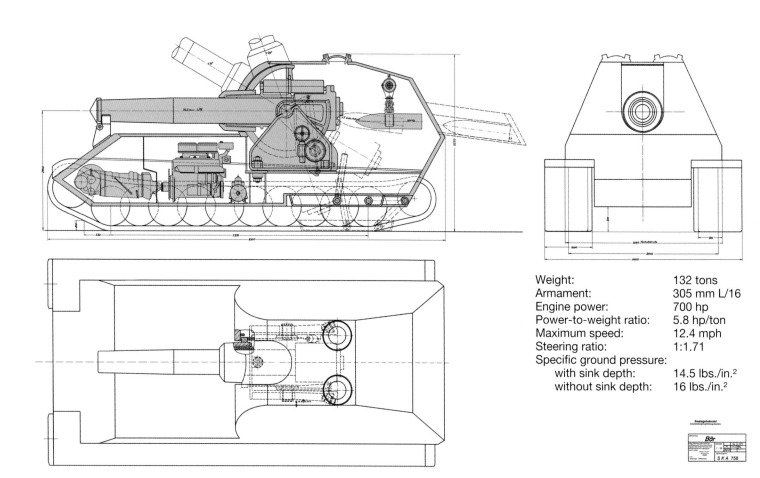

Weight:	132 tons
Armament:	305 mm L/16
Engine power:	700 hp
Power-to-weight ratio:	5.8 hp/ton
Maximum speed:	12.4 mph
Steering ratio:	1:1.71
Specific ground pressure:	
with sink depth:	14.5 lbs./in.²
without sink depth:	16 lbs./in.²

with rubber inserts. Unlike the suspensions of the *Tiger* and *Panther*, this vehicle had a leaf suspension. Apart from the vehicle's low height, the main reason for this decision may have been the removable base plate in the rear of the vehicle. The use of transverse torsion bars would have interfered with this brace, which was supposed to absorb the 175-ton recoil. This armored howitzer had a weight of 132 tons, which the 120 hp of the Maybach gasoline engine was supposed to accelerate to about 12 mph. The vehicle's dimensions consisted of a length of 322 inches, a width of 161 inches,

and a height of 140 inches. Since these dimensions (especially the width) exceeded railroad limits, 20-inch-wide transport tracks were envisaged instead of the 3.9-inch-wide battle tracks. With a track contact area of 209 inches, the battle tracks resulted in the relatively high ground pressure of 16 psi on a firm surface. With a sink depth of 7.9 inches, the increased track contact area of 232 inches resulted in a halfway acceptable ground pressure of 14.50 psi. With the track gauge of 122 inches, steering ratio was 1:1.71.

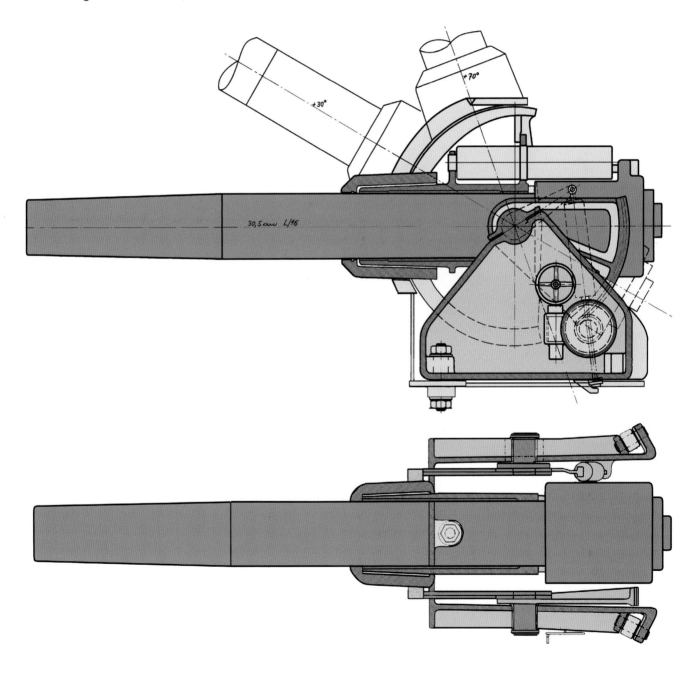

The *Panzermörser Bär*'s frontal armor consisted of an upper plate with a thickness of 5.1 inches and a 3.9-inch lower plate. The vehicle's side armor was 3.1 inches thick and the roof armor 2 inches. For protection against mines, floor armor was envisaged as 2.35 inches in the front and 1.2 inches in the rear. The crew of six had two different types of ammunition for the 17.5-ton gun, whose weight was made up of the 8.8-ton gun barrel, 6.6-ton carriage, and a 2.5-ton armored shield:

The soft-steel prototype of the *Sturmtiger*, a 380 mm howitzer mounted on the chassis of the *Panzerkampfwagen VI Tiger* (*Sd.Kfz. 181*) by Alkett Berlin. Hitler inspected this armored howitzer at a demonstration of new weapons on October 20, 1943. *Hoffmann Collection-Bavarian State Library Munich*

- a concrete shell weighing 838 lbs., with 77 lbs. of explosives, initial velocity of 1,132 fps, and maximum firing range of 6.2 miles.
- a high-explosive shell weighing 771 lbs., with 110 lbs. of explosives, initial velocity of 1,164 fps, and maximum firing range of 6.5 miles.

Maximum barrel recoil was 39 inches. Aiming angles were 0 to 70 degrees in elevation with 4 degrees of traverse (2 degrees to each side).

In this regard the *Wa Prüf* 4/II officer informed Dr. Müller about the development of an assault gun based on the *Tiger* I by Alkett Berlin (with Altmärkische Kettenwerke, a subsidiary of Rheinmetall-Borsig). The vehicle was armed with a naval gun with a caliber of 380 mm and a firing range of 3.5 miles.

Dr. Müller admitted that he was unfamiliar with this vehicle development but was not surprised, since Alkett was typically less involved with new developments, instead, as a rule, combining existing devices. As well, Alkett projects were generally guided by the authority of the Army Ordnance Office directly from the Reich Ministry for Armaments and War Production; namely, by *Amtsleiter* Saur. The responsible *Waffenamt* officer from *Wa Prüf* 4/II was of the opinion that the Krupp development represented the future, more harmonic vehicle; however, at that time (on May 19, 1943) there were no military requirements for the design and production of such a vehicle.[33]

Nevertheless, Hitler and his armaments ministry desired and had ideas for extremely heavy guns, into which Krupp, always interested in new developments, was ready to delve. While the company had at least kept the Army Ordnance Office, specifically *Wa Prüf* 6/II, informed about the *Panzermörser Bär* project, despite the tremendous material and personnel costs, the project for an even-heavier armored howitzer seems to have completely slipped past the Army Ordnance Office. Since the planned materials allocations went through *Hauptamtsleiter* Saur, the development launch must have been Hitler's decision, because of the close relationship between Karl-Otto Saur and Hitler. As an example, reference must again be made to the conversation mentioned in the previous chapter between Saur and Hitler at a demonstration of new weapons, including the *Maus* model, on May 14, 1943. Had Edward Grote and Director Hacker issued a development contract for a large armored vehicle,

Grote would have recognized the superficial and in part faulty design work and assigned further work to an experienced and inventive company: the Krupp company of Essen.

While Edward Grote's 1,100-ton tank was the result of hypotheses and rough estimates, Krupp went significantly further with its designs for superheavy armored howitzers. This company had gained experience in the development and construction of such large vehicles with the construction and design of the *Maus* tank and the previously mentioned R-2 mobile coastal gun mount.

Given the large area of North Sea coastline that had to be defended, the *Kriegsmarine*, traditionally responsible for coastal defense, saw in the development of motorized coastal artillery a way to react quickly to attacks from the sea. In addition to the 150 mm C/28 motorized fast-firing cannon, interest also grew in making even-larger guns mobile for coastal defense. The result entailed projects for a 380 mm gun called the R-1, the previously mentioned 280 mm gun named the R-2, the 240 mm gun named the R-3, and the 203 mm gun named the R-4, all four of which were on tracked carriages. Of these projects, only the R-2 project reached the prototype construction phase. The gun to be used was the 280 mm C/34 rapid-firing cannon with a barrel length of L/54.5.

In design and performance, this gun was similar to the 280 mm guns on the battleships *Scharnhorst* and *Gneisenau*. A muzzle brake was envisaged for the R-2 self-propelled carriage to reduce recoil. In addition to the 43.5-ton gun barrel with threaded breech, Krupp also planned a 44-ton barrel with threaded breech. When planning began in 1942, as described in the previous chapter, the vehicle was to be powered by a twelve-cylinder Maybach gasoline engine with a six-speed transmission with reduction. This was to enable the roughly 143-ton vehicle to reach a maximum speed of 14 mph. For rail transport, two individual four-axle bogies were selected, between which the vehicle was to be slung, similar to the 600 mm *Karl* howitzer and the French Char 2c breakthrough tank.

In order to remain within railroad-loading dimensions, the crew had to pull back the 280 mm gun barrel about 40 inches in the direction of the engine compartment, replace the 39-inch-wide battle tracks with 28-inch-wide loading tracks, and, again analogous to the *Karl* 600 mm howitzer, retract the running gear. Unlike the *Karl*, however, this was not accomplished mechanically but by means of hydraulic

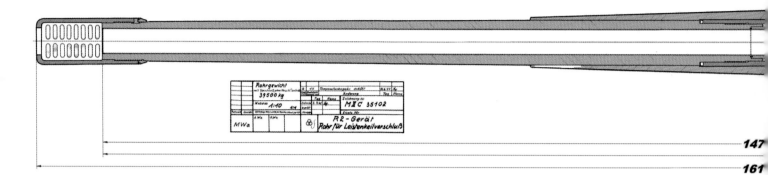

147

161

The two breech variants of the 280 mm L/54.5 gun, which was to have been used in the R-2 self-propelled carriage

cylinders. To do this, the crew operated the wheel mountings, then called "air shocks." This term cannot be entirely correct, for in today's parlance it would have had to be a type of hydropneumatic suspension. The two loose-hanging tracks could be lashed down.

The howitzer was to be fired from a 24-ton revolving bed, which allowed the gun to be traversed 360 degrees. Krupp envisaged a simplified ammunition lift for loading the ammunition. The projectile, the precartridge, and the main cartridge were transported from the ammunition compartment one after the other. The gun crew pushed the ammunition into the gun's loading space with the aid of a hydraulically operated rammer.[34]

Development of this vehicle lagged; because of its low priority, Krupp could not plan construction of a prototype R-2 until the first half of 1944, which was later postponed until September 1944. The positive experiences resulting from designing the running-gear design of the *Maus* tank

resulted in the adoption of the complete transmission-drive concept of the diesel engine–generator–electric-motor principle. Krupp envisaged using the MB 507 diesel engine used to power the navy's *Schnellboote* (motor torpedo boats), which was already succeeding in service in the *Karl* 600 mm howitzer, also called the *Gerät* 040.

Krupp was supposed to complete nine-tenths of the prototype of the R-2 self-propelled carriage in the production area at Essen. After completion, its place was to be taken by an even more gigantic combat vehicle, the 1,100-ton *Urling* armored howitzer. The surviving files do not reveal out of what necessity this monster was to be produced and used. The fact is that the project took place on behalf of the armaments ministry and thus at Hitler's direction. Questions about its tactical usefulness can be answered only by its use against heavily fortified positions, of which after the fall of the Soviet fortress of Sevastopol and the French Maginot Line only the British fortress of Gibraltar remained. To this

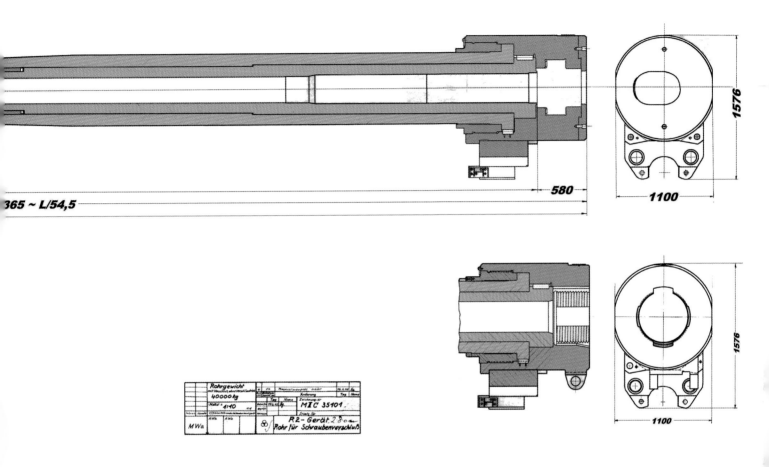

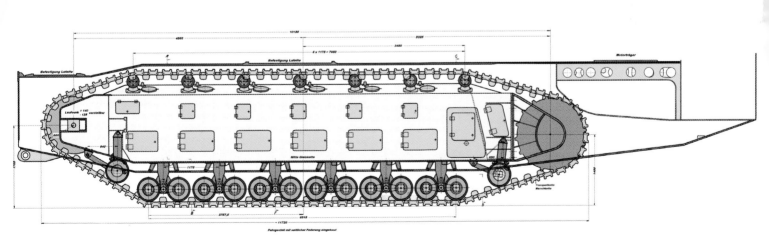

Side view of the R-2 suspension without engine-generator and without the 280 mm gun. In the drawing the driver's position is facing in the direction of travel. The propulsion system and drive sprocket are present in the drawing at right. The device thus moved forward, with the gun barrel leading the way.

R 2

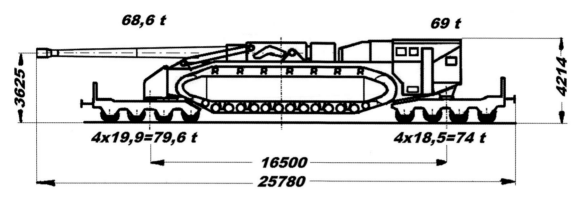

68,6 t   69 t

3625   4214

4x19,9=79,6 t   4x18,5=74 t

16500

25780

Verlastet auf Schiene
mit zurückgezogenen Geschütz

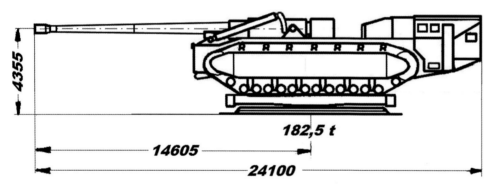

4355

182,5 t

14605

24100

Feuerstellung auf Drehscheibe

The individual movement and position variants of the R-2 coastal self-propelled carriage

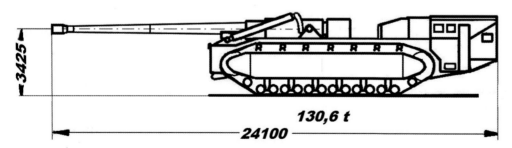

3425

130,6 t

24100

Fahr- und Feuerstellung

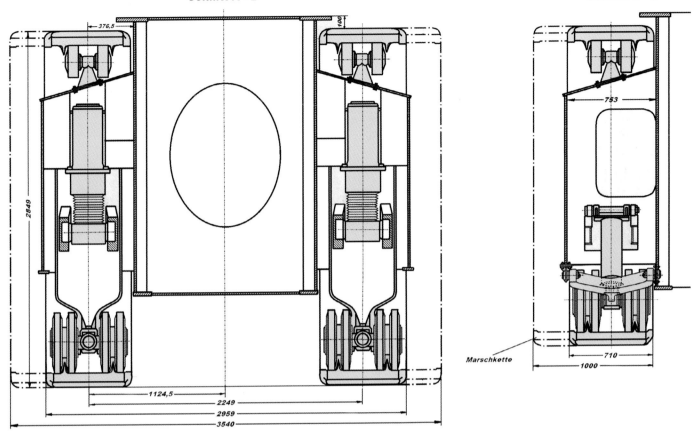

Schnitt A - B

376,5
100
2849
1124,5
2249
2959
3540

Schnitt C - D

753
710
1000

Marschkette

Cross sections A–B and C–D through the running gear of the R-2 self-propelled carriage, which clearly illustrate the wheel mounting principle

Details of the running-gear lashing, which was considered necessary for transport by rail in order to maintain the necessary distance between tracks and the railroad-loading standard

Zurrung der Gleiskette auf Eisenbahn

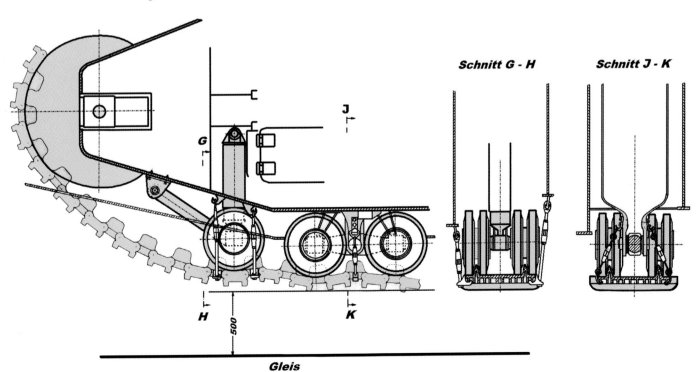

Schnitt G - H

Schnitt J - K

G
J
H
K
500

Gleis

end, the necessary bogies for the *Dora* 800 mm gun and the low-loaders for the *Maus* tank had already been made in "Spanish gauge." The superheavy gun armament, the heavy frontal armor, and the heavy close-range armament gave presumptions free rein. Use in an urban area such as Stalingrad could not be optimal for this weapon because of its huge size, especially since its climbing ability would have been anything but ideal. While there are only rough sketches and models of Edward Grote's big tanks, starting in February 4, 1943, Krupp, an experienced German company, produced designs of this gigantic howitzer project that were planned and developed most accurately. The first two preliminary designs depicted two different large vehicles.

The first armored howitzer had an 800 mm gun and was the origin of the legend of a 1,500-ton tank with the well-known 800 mm *Kanone (E) Dora*, which to this day remains the largest gun ever made. In recent years, several fantasy drawings have been produced that have nothing to do with reality. The *Dora* gun had a barrel length of 1,280 inches, equal to a caliber length of L/40, while the 800 mm armored howitzer had a barrel length of 427 inches. The *Dora's* gun barrel weighed 440 tons, while that of the armored howitzer weighed 164 tons. The initial velocity of the concrete shell fired by the 800 mm *Kanone (E) Dora* gun was 2,362 fps, but only 1,150 fps when fired by the armored howitzer, since as a high-angle gun it was not designed for the longest possible range.

The only commonality between the planned 800 mm armored howitzer and the existing *Dora* 800 mm gun was the ammunition, or to be more accurate, the shells to be used, which consisted of the available 7.7-ton concrete shells and the 5.3-ton high-explosive shells, which had already been used by the 800 mm *Kanone (E) Dora*. In addition, in keeping with the nature of the gun, it was envisaged that another howitzer shell with a weight of 6.6 tons and an initial velocity of 492 fps would be developed. Correspondingly,

An interesting size comparison between the 800 mm *Dora* gun and the people in front of it during a demonstration of the new weapon at Rügenwalde (East Prussia) on April 3, 1943

the planned muzzle energy was just 6,900 meters per ton (mt). The big armored howitzer was also to have a flak turret and a flamethrower. Krupp also envisaged the installation of mine rollers, similar to those of a Soviet project (see the previous chapter). Dimensions were so gigantic that estimated weight was 1,984 tons, even though the vehicle's dimensions were smaller than those of Edward Grote's P-1000 tank. Compared to the Grote tank, however, the armored howitzer was seriously underpowered, which expressed itself in the maximum achievable speed, comparable to a walking pace.

The vehicle's planned power-to-weight ratio was just 4.46 hp per ton, or 6.74 hp per ton compared to the Grote

tank's respectable 64 hp per ton. One could therefore describe the armored howitzer as a self-propelled, heavily armored gun. The "smaller" of the two variants had a 600 mm howitzer and a weight of 880 tons. This caliber had also been used by the *Karl* 600 mm howitzer, also called *Gerät* 040, which had been built in small numbers by Rheinmetall following a similar concept of operation. The tables include a comparison of technical data.

The main difference between the 600 mm *Karl* howitzer and the planned 600 or 800 mm Krupp howitzers was the former's lack of armor. This made the *Gerät* 040 vulnerable to fire from enemy artillery and aircraft. The two armored howitzers

Hitler, Dr. Müller, and *Hauptamtsleiter* Saur beside the 7-ton concrete shell for the *Dora* gun, an 800 mm version of which Krupp envisaged for the armored howitzer

planned by Krupp were to have very thick 7.9-inch roof armor, which offered effective protection against direct artillery hits and air attacks. These extraordinary armor thicknesses also provided defense against mines, with 5.9 inches of floor armor in the forward section of the armored howitzer.

In May 1943, Krupp had decided in favor of the smaller 600 mm howitzer, incorporating features of the 800 mm howitzer such as the flamethrower, which drove the planned combat weight to over 1,100 tons. The production version of the 600 mm howitzer was given the code name *Urling*, which, as already described in the introduction, roughly means "a figure from the past who is rooted in the past." Other well-known companies were drawn into the design and production effort, including Daimler-Benz AG, Siemens-Schuckert-Werke AG, Robert Bosch GmbH, Waggonbau Wegemann & Co., Voight Eberspächter, Poppe AG, Klatte, and Mann Hummel GmbH.

Because of the special secrecy level, the individual segments of the howitzer design were given special code names. The planned *Urling* armored howitzer consisted of the following such names:

■ The **Veilchen** (Violet) device, which included the complete power train. Daimler-Benz was responsible for the diesel engines and their controls. The electrical parts of the drive system, such as the double generators, the electric motors, and their controls, were known to the Siemens-Schuckert company only under the term *Kran 43* device. Krupp was responsible for the engine housing and armor.

■ The **Schiller** device, which was the project for the companies responsible for development of the necessary hydraulic systems for aiming and loading the howitzer, the outer flaps, and design of the bridges. The work had an equal impact both on the *Veilchen* and *Lindwurm* projects.

■ The **Lindwurm** (Dragon) project, which for example required Wegemann & Co. to produce two flamethrowers with a range of 295 ft. The design of the armored superstructure and the running gear fell into Krupp's area of responsibility, while the Siemens-Schuckert-Werke was supposed to provide the four drive motors.

The file numbers could give a reader with no knowledge of the project only a vague idea of the connection that existed. The secrecy effort functioned so well that even today, not much is known about this gigantic project. So far, no detailed sources concerning the vehicle's main armament, the 600 mm

	600 mm Armored Howitzer	600 mm *Gerät* 040 Karl
Weight	801 tons	120 tons
Power-to-weight ratio	6.74 hp/ton	5.8 hp/ton
Barrel length	L/21, equivalent to 40.35'	L/8.44
Barrel weight	90 tons	28.4 tons
Maximum speed	5 mph	6 mph
Ground pressure	23 lbs./in.²	25 lbs./in.²
Steering ratio	1:1.8	1:2.64
Range	8.7 miles	2.5 miles
Armor	9.8" to 3.9"	0.47"
Shell weight	3.0 tons	2.2 tons
Initial velocity	1,280 fps	721 fps
Recoil	1,000 tons	500 tons
Muzzle energy	23,300 mt	5,400 mt

Krupp Files	V 251-1	V-253-1
Code Name	*Urling* Basic	*Urling* Materials
	G/2083 293	G/2084 294
MA Internal Archive No.	RH8/v 2986 changed to 2987	RH8/v 2979
V 25 a-1	**V 25 d-1**	**V 25 e-1**
Veilchen Device	**Schiller Device**	**Lindwurm Device**
G/2080 290	G/2081 291	G/2082 292
RH8/v 2980	RH8/v 2978	RH8/v 2985
Power House	**Girders**	**Housing**
Armor	Armor	Armor
Iron Construction	Iron Construction	Side Armor
Hydraulic Doors	Bolt Connection	Iron Construction
Floor Hatch	Mounting of Girders	Exhaust
Hydraulics	Accessibility	
Floor Hatch	Seals	**Running Gear**
Ammunition Elevator	Air Channels	Mechanical Running Gear
	Air Filter	Air Suspension
Machinery		Drive Sprocket with Gearing
Integrated Motors	**Hydraulic Systems**	Track Tensioner
Exhaust Systems	Pumps	Brakes
Fuel Lines	Accumulators	
Cooling water pipes	Battery pack	**Electrical System**
Oil Systems	Fluid Reservoirs	**with Drive**
Air Lines	Air Bottles	Installation of Driving Motors
Intermediate Gearing	Elevation Mechanism Control	Ventilation of Driving Motors
Bilge Pump System	Lines	Cable Joints
Electrical System	**Electrical System**	**Flamethrower and**
(for SSW of the Kran 43)	Electrical Installations	**and Machine Gun Positions**
Integrated Generators		Flamethrower Spray Head
Driving Switch	**Ammunition Loading**	Flamethrower Pumps
Control Stick	Loader	Flamethrower Piping
Brake Drive	Elevator	Flamethrower Controls
Clutch Drive	Lifting Gear	MG Position Forward
Throttle and Starter Rods	Troughs	MG Position Center
Switchboard		MG Position Rear
Telescope System		

howitzer, have been found. There is, however, the possibility that the missing lowercase letters *b* and *c* (V 25 b-1 and V 25 c-1) in the Krupp file numbering stand for these still-missing documents.

With dimensions of 866 inches (length) by 350 inches (width) by 7275 inches (height), the *Urling* armored howitzer was more compactly designed than the Grote tank. A consequence of this was surely the armored howitzer's relatively small propulsion system, which consisted of eight Daimler-Benz MB 507 torpedo boat engines in combination with four double generators. This combination corresponded exactly to the principle of combination that Porsche had designed for the Porsche type 205 (*Maus* tank). There were, however, differences in diesel engine output and electrical data of the generators and drive motors.

In the *Maus* tank (chassis number 205 002), one supercharged MB 512 diesel engine with an output of 1,200 hp and a speed of 2,400 rpm drove a directly coupled double generator with an output of 2 × 450 kW at 800 volts. The two drive motors produced 415 kW at 775 volts and a speed of 1,160 rpm. The maximum speed of the motors was 3,000 rpm. Both aggregate types required an energizing voltage of 48 volts.

In the case of the *Urling* armored howitzer, two MB 507 diesel engines, each producing 800 hp at 2,200 rpm and coupled by means of an intermediate gearbox, drove a double generator with an output of 2 × 450 kW at 900 volts. Siemens-Schuckert envisaged an energizing voltage of 110 Volts. With the help of the intermediate gearbox, the double generators reached a speed of 2,600 rpm. As a result of an electrical efficiency of 93.7 percent and because of the power consumption of the auxiliary drives, a total available output at the drive motors was just 3,392 kW (4,612 hp), with a combined diesel output of 4,700 kW (6,400 hp) via a double-generator total output of 3,600 kW. As a result, the achievable power-to-weight ratio of the *Urling* armored heavy howitzer was only 6.1 hp per ton, compared to which the *Maus* tank had a slightly superior power-to-weight ratio of 6.35 hp per ton. By comparison, the 75-ton *Tiger* II, with its 700 hp Maybach engine, had a power-to-weight ratio of 10.3 hp per ton and was still underpowered.

Another difference resulted from the internal-combustion engines used. The power-to-weight ratio of an MB 507 diesel engine was 1.75 lbs. per hp at maximum power, and with the add-on components it achieved a value of 1.80 lbs. per hp. By comparison, the twelve-cylinder Maybach HL 230 gasoline engine, the standard power plant of the German *Tiger* and *Panther* heavy tanks, had a power-to-weight ratio of 3.75 lbs. per hp with an engine weight of 2,645 lbs. and a maximum output of 700 hp.

	Maus Tank Electrical System	*Urling* Armored Howitzer Electrical System
Double generator output	2 x 450 kW	2 x 450 kW
Maximum RPM	2,600	2,600
Nominal voltage	560 volts	
Maximum voltage	800 volts	900 volts
Excitation or also Field voltage	48 volts	110 volts
Excitation machine output	18 kW at 375 A	2 kW
Voltage	48 volts	110 volts
Electric motor output	415 kW at 1,160 rpm	848 kW at 1,900 rpm
Maximum RPM	3,000	3,000
Maximum voltage	775 volts	900 volts
Nominal voltage	550 volts	
Excitation or also Field voltage	48 volts	110 volts

46227

One of the eight MB 507 *Schnellboot* diesel engines (still equipped with gear units for ship generators), which distinguished themselves through their very light construction

46231

Specification for the MB 507 *Schnellboot* Engine

V-engine with	2 × 6 cylinders
Compression ratio	1:17
Bore/stroke	6.4 × 7"
Displacement per cylinder	225.8 in.^{3}
Total displacement	2,715 in.^{3}
Torque at continuous power	275.5 mkg
Fuel consumption at continuous power	180 gal./PS/h
March power	650 hp at 1,730 rpm
Continuous power	750 hp at 1,950 rpm
Full power	850 hp at 2,200 rpm
Maximum power	1,000 hp at 2,400 rpm
Dimensions	72 inches long, 31 inches wide, 41.7 inches high
Weight	1,741 lbs. (without accessories) and 1,808 lbs. complete

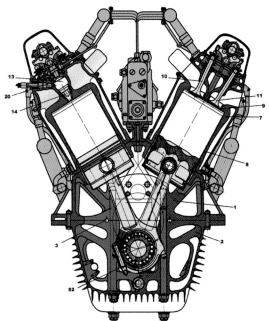
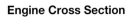

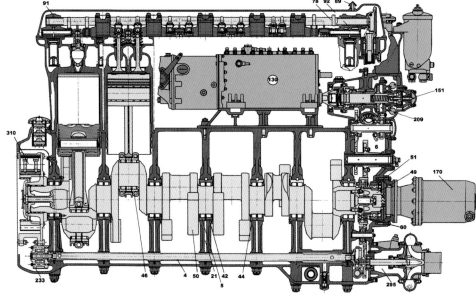

Engine Cross Section

1 Crankcase upper part
2 Crankcase lower part
3 Crankcase fit roller
7 Cylinder
8 Cylinder liner
9 Valve seat
10 Inlet valve
11 Outlet valve
13 Front chamber
14 Burner
20 Spark plugs
52 Radial engine oil hole

Engine Longitudinal Section

4 Engine oil distributor shaft
5 Crankcase bearing
6 Great train power unit
21 Crankshaft bearing for engine oil hole
42 Axial engine oil hole
44 Crankshaft mount without engine oil hole
45 Crankshaft
46 Pushrod bearing
49 Starter claw on the crankshaft
50 Counterweight
51 Axial thrust bearing on the crankshaft
60 Elastic drive wheel

78 Right camshaft
89 Ventilator
91 Camshaft bearing 1
92 Camshaft bearing block for engine oil hole
130 Fuel oil pump group
150 Alternator (not shown, above 170)
151 Remote RPM counter
170 Pressure gas starter
209 Injection start adjustment
233 Engine oil pressure feed pump, lower part of crankcase
295 Fresh coolant pump
310 Engine clutch

These eight Daimler-Benz diesel engines had been divided into two levels. For vibration reasons, a machine deck consisted of engines with clockwise and counterclockwise directions of rotation, since the direction of rotation of the diesel engines could be easily changed. Each two cooperative diesel engines, responsible for a double generator, were one above the other. Two individual generators powered one of the four electric drive motors. These drive motors sat on one drive sprocket and, at a maximum voltage of 900 volts and a maximum speed of 1,900 rpm, each produced 848 kW.

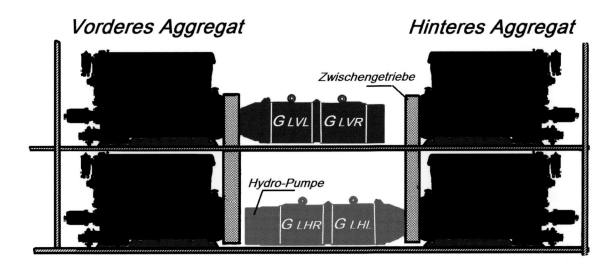

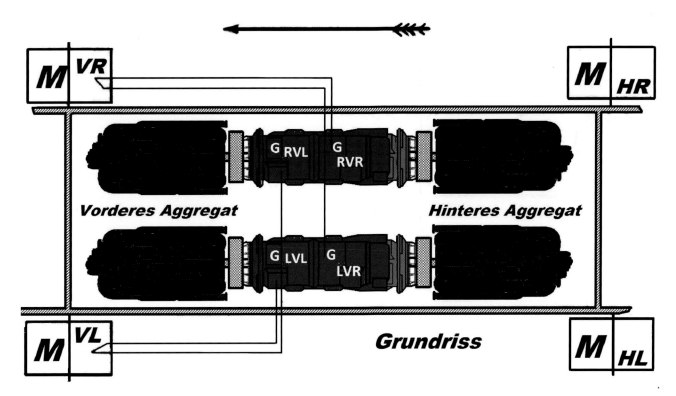

The outline and layout of the propulsion system, which to maintain secrecy was code-named *"Veilchen Device"* or *"Kran 43."*

Siemens-Schuckert had also developed a special drive scheme: each two diesel engines powered an electric motor, so that propulsion, though slower, was still possible if a diesel engine was lost. For example the first individual generator (G-LVL) of the front-left upper double generator and the first individual generator (G-RVL) of the front-right upper double generator together powered the front-left drive motor (M-VL). The right-side drive motor received its propulsion from the two rear individual generators (G-LVR and G-RVR). In this scheme, the two lower double generators powered the two rear drive motors (see drawing), the left-rear motor by the LHL and RHL generators and the right-rear motor by the LHR and RHR generators.

Analogous to the *Maus* tank, all double generators also had a flange-mounted auxiliary generator. These auxiliary generators (also called "excitation devices" in the documents) produced a voltage of 110 volts at an output of 2 kW. As the name suggests, these generators served to excite the main generators and drive motors. The main dimensions of the machine unit, or the double generator without ventilation opening, were about 90.5 inches in length and 33 inches in diameter.

In addition to the auxiliary generators, these two lower double generators also had two flange-mounted hydraulic main pumps, which by way of the pressure accumulators, or *Akkus*, were supposed to supply the hydraulic consumers (also see *Schiller* device). Cooling of the double generators and the drive motors was accomplished with the aid of fans. On the end input shaft end of each double generator there was a powerful fan that blew cooling air through a jacket to the center of the machine unit, from where it was then distributed (as in the *Maus* tank). The diesel engines, in contrast, had a liquid cooling system, which in addition to the double water pumps consisted of a total of twelve radiators. Two diesel engines shared one radiator. The other radiators served the separate exhaust and oil coolers and the two constant-voltage machine units. In order to draw the hot air out of the radiator compartments, twenty ventilators were installed, which required an output of 400 hp. They were driven by auxiliary shafts coming from the intermediate gearing. Daimler-Benz achieved the connection between diesel engine and double generator by using a MAN-Renk clutch.

Because the electrical system was controlled by means of a Leonard set, two machine units with constant-voltage generators were installed to produce the control voltage. They produced a maximum output of 60 kW at 110 volts.

These generators were independent of the main power plants and were powered by two four-cylinder diesel engines, each producing 80 hp at 2,600 rpm. Since Daimler-Benz was incapable of supplying these, either Borgward or Hanomag was envisaged as supplier. This principle was similar to the circuitry used in the *Maus* tank, in which the two small diesel engines, which powered the coupled direct-current generators, were started first. These generators were thus able to power the four auxiliary generators mounted on the double generators, which in this case functioned as motors. The power thus generated was therefore able to start the twelve-cylinder diesel engines connected to the double generators. Since two engines were always permanently connected by intermediate gearing, two diesel engines could always be started simultaneously. The standard practice was to start the engines with compressed air. Daimler-Benz had envisaged a compressed-air starter system that was to be attached directly to the MB 507 diesel engine.

The engines also had an amalgamated operating panel, from where the starter wiring led to the air distributors on the cylinder blocks. For each two diesel engines there were four compressed-air bottles, each with a capacity of 26 liters. In addition, the diesel engines had flange-mounted compressors to charge the compressed-air bottles. Starting the diesel engines with compressed air also had the advantage that because of the common gearing, excess energy could be stored in the rigidly connected rotors of the generators, making it easier to start the engines. To charge the batteries of the 24-volt electrical system, Daimler-Benz had equipped the eight MB 507 diesel engines with flange-mounted 24-volt GQLM 1000/24 alternators. The cooling air filters used for the diesel engines were Mann-Hummel filters with 120 axial cells. Since the envisaged intake height was about 16.25 ft. (5 m) above the ground, the developers presumed that relatively clean air would be drawn in, so that thought could be given to doing away with the planned cyclone filter and instead using a simpler wet air filter.

The four DW 307701 drive motors required a nominal voltage of 625 volts, with the highest possible armature voltage being 900 volts. By means of an excitation voltage of 110 volts and an output of 5 kW, these motors achieved a nominal current of 1,600 amperes. After the deduction of losses, the output power per motor was 845 kW. The electric motors transmitted the power to the 52.75-inch drive sprockets

The photos and the drawing show the GV-305/30 800-volt double generator made by Siemens-Schuckert for the *Maus* tank. It produced 3 × 450 kW. The double generator used in the *Urling* armored howitzer was similar in design, but because of its higher output of 2 × 450 kW at 900 volts, it was somewhat larger than the one in the *Maus* tank. In this case, Siemens-Schuckert flange-mounted a 110-volt auxiliary generator in place of the 48-volt GV-295/13 in the *Maus*. The auxiliary generator created excitation voltage for the generator and electric motors.

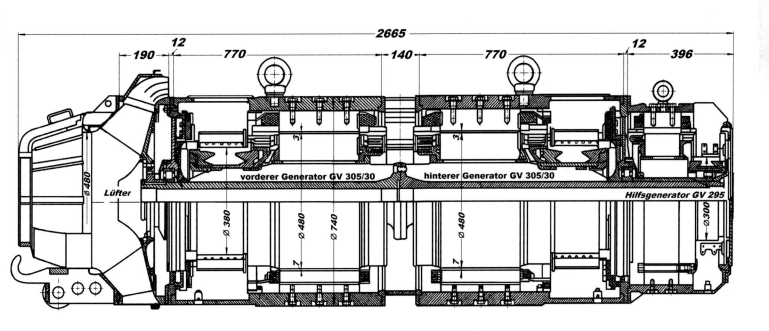

Weighing 1.87 tons, this D-2185 driving motor made by Siemens-Schuckert was from the *Maus* tank. Running on 800 volts, this motor produced 415 kW at 1,160 rpm. The motor's maximum speed was 3,100 rpm. Electrical efficiency was 93.7%.

by means of four drive sprocket transmissions with a ratio of 1:47.8. A transmission ratio of 1:51 had been envisaged, which would have required a 56-inch drive sprocket.

Maximum total pulling force was 1,090 tons at a speed of 0.6 mph. This meant a maximum pulling force of 248 tons for each individual track. At the maximum possible speed of 6 mph, total pulling power was still 118 tons. Krupp installed a hydraulic parking brake on each of the drive motors. Operation of the four drum brakes was by means of the existing hydraulic system from the Schiller project. Because of their proximity to the electric motors, these brakes were supposed to be used only when the vehicle was stopped, if at all possible, so as to avoid the transmission of thermal problems and possible damage to the drive motor bearings.

Krupp and Siemens-Schuckert envisaged an electric braking system like the one tested on the *Maus* tank. The engineers planned that braking would be fully automatic as soon as the drive motors were powered from the vehicle; there was no need for the driver to adjust the speed regulator. The energy produced was saved by the double generators, now functioning as electric motors.

The coupled diesel engines thus worked as compressors, and the resulting compressed air was supposed to be forced through the outlet valves. The internal friction of the operating diesel engines also helped achieve the desired braking performance. The braking power of the MB 507 diesel engine with the engine switched off was about 200 hp at 2,300 rpm. To prevent the engine from overrevving, the diesel engine had a speed governor on the Bosch injection pump, keeping it within the required speed range of 450 to 2,300 rpm by restricting the amount of fuel injected into the engine. If the engine was idling, maximum braking power per engine was 140 hp, while with the engine shut down, with no fuel injection, 200 hp could be achieved as described. Since the ancillary components also had internal friction, the following picture resulted:

- 330 hp braking power for two diesel engines, including their fans
- 30 hp braking power for the fan of a double generator
- 33 hp braking power for the fan of a drive motor, including the losses in the constant-voltage machine units (18 kW)

- 6 hp braking power for the generators' excitation power
- 10 hp braking power for a drive motor's excitation power

This resulted in a total braking power of 409 hp per machine unit and thus 1,636 hp for the entire system. Engine speed monitoring was considered particularly important, so that while driving uphill, for example, the diesel engines did not overspeed. The designers wanted to use a centrifugal switch in addition to a warning lamp. The Professor Porsche KG had developed a very small centrifugal switch for the *Maus* tank, in which Krupp and Siemens-Schuckert displayed great interest. These switches were supposed to be mounted on the double generators and on the drive motors and react at a generator speed of 3,000 rpm, which corresponded to the maximum diesel engine speed of 2,550 rpm, which could be used for a maximum of five minutes. If this was exceeded, the hydraulic brakes were activated and the fuel feed cut back.

The drive motor response speed was 2,330 rpm. The hydraulic brakes were not supposed to be released until all rpm were within limits. This automatic operation ultimately did not meet with approval, because the reduction of diesel engine power until the brakes were released was undesirable. And so the warning lamp remained. If the lamp illuminated, the driver was supposed to leave the drive regulator where it was and brake mechanically until the lamp went out again.

The driver's instrument panel, more accurately an instrument table, was impressively large, with

- one rpm indicator for each diesel engine, for a total of eight instruments;
- one oil pressure gauge for each diesel engine, for a total of eight instruments;
- one air pressure manometer for intake air per diesel engine, for a total of eight instruments;
- one coolant temperature gauge for each diesel engine, for a total of eight instruments;
- one oil temperature gauge for each diesel engine, for a total of eight instruments;
- one fuel gauge for each diesel engine, for a total of eight instruments;
- two pyrometers (radiation thermometers for exhaust cooling) per diesel engine, for a total of sixteen instruments; and

- one preheating switch for the glow plugs per diesel engine, for a total of eight switches.

This meant sixty-four instruments for monitoring the Daimler-Benz diesel engines alone, not to mention the electrical-system instruments such as volt and amp meters and various warning lights, which can be retraced on the basis of the example of the *Maus* tank. Each generator had a volt meter for the armature voltage, an ampere meter for the armature current, and an ampere meter for the excitation. There was also an ampere meter for the exciting current of the drive motor. With eight generators and four motors, this meant an additional twenty-eight instruments. Missing from the general instrumentation was a tachometer (the *Maus* had a tachometer for each track side), charging current indicator for the batteries, an inclinometer, and the usual heading indicator. The vehicle driver had about 100 instruments in front of him, making it necessary to plan the use of an onboard mechanic.

The next subfield of the *Urling* design was the 600 mm *Mörser* L/20.5, about which, unfortunately, not much more information could be found. Design of the heavy howitzer was based on that for a 600 mm *Mörser* with the code name *Ulrich*. Development of this gun began in mid-1943 on the basis of a 600 mm gun designated Device 36. The short-barreled heavy howitzer with a barrel length of L/8 was supposed to fire a 1.65-ton shell with a muzzle velocity of 820 fps. The L/8 gun barrel weighed 33 tons. In comparison, the gun barrel of the planned *Urling* 600 mm howitzer with a barrel length of L/20.5 weighed 89 tons. Its cradle had four recoil brakes and a recuperator cylinder, whose task it was to limit recoil to 59 inches. The recoil force on the flange was 1,430 tons. The hydraulically powered elevation gear made possible an elevation range of 0 to 70 degrees. Ammunition delivery by means of an elevator, operation of the breech, and the machine for loading the ammunition were all hydraulic. Ammunition capacity was to be eight rounds, which would be stored in a sort of magazine.

This design sector fell into the project branch of the *Schiller* device. The hydraulic system consisted of two main pumps with a maximum output each of 0.8 gallons per second at a speed of 500 rpm. The pumps were powered by secondary drives on the two lower double generators. The hydraulic pumps produced a delivery pressure of 1,700 to 1,990 psi. To provide reserves for sudden consumption

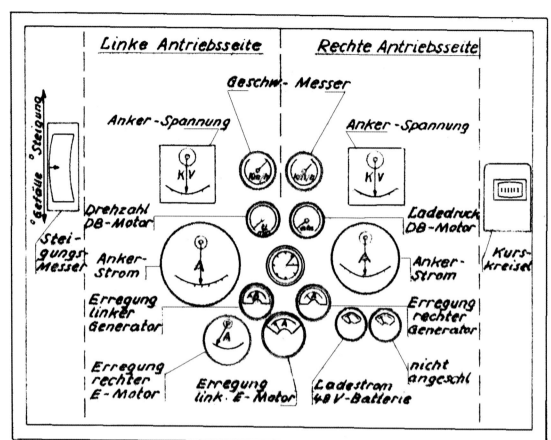

Here as an example, the auxiliary instrument panel from the *Maus* I for just one double generator. One can assume that these instruments from Siemens would also have been used in the *Urling*, arranged for eight double generators and four electric driving motors.

spikes, the engineers used two pressure tanks, which were referred to as *Akkus* in the period documents. This planned hydraulic system had to supply the following users:

- the elevation mechanism
- the breech
- the loader
- the ammunition lift
- the floor hatch
- the sliding door in the rear wall
- the armored skirts
- the flamethrower
- the brakes

The *Lindwurm* device represented another project branch. As can be seen from the summary, the project consisted of the armored housing, the mechanical running gear with air suspension, the drive sprocket with transmission, the track tensioners, and the foot and parking brakes. Construction of the running gear included the installation of the four electric drive motors. The running gear and tracks very closely resembled those of the *Maus* tank. The diameter of one of the *Urling*'s 128 road wheels was 21 inches, while those of the *Maus* were 21.6 inches in diameter. The track width of a single track was 46.25 inches for the *Urling* armored howitzer and 43.3 inches for the *Maus* tank. Maximum load on a road wheel when the vehicle was moving was supposed to be 8.9 tons; Krupp estimated a maximum load of 14.5 tons per road wheel during firing.

In addition to the machine gun positions that were part of the project, the companies also had to install the flamethrower system. Contractor for the flamethrower system was Waggonfabrik Wegmann & Co. AG of Kassel. The company had gained experience in the construction of flamethrowers through the building of the *Flammpanzer* II on the chassis of the *Panzer* II. It had two flamethrowers in small rotating turrets on the track shields, which with a range of rotation of 180 degrees achieved a flame jet range of 115 ft. After problems, especially during street fighting in Stalingrad, a *Flammpanzer* III was built, based on the *Panzer* III. In this case, Wegmann installed a flame tube in the mount for the coaxial MG34, which had been removed. The flame tube had a 0.55-inch nozzle, which was covered by an outer sleeve. The system used a 264-gallon flame oil tank.

The pressure buildup of 213 psi was achieved by means of a 1.1-liter DKW two-stroke engine. Instead of the requested flame jet range of 180 ft., in practice only 115 ft. could be achieved. Therefore, on April 9, 1943, discussions were held in Kassel between representatives of Krupp and Wegmann & Co. about a new flamethrower design. Krupp proposed the use of the existing hydraulic-system pressure tanks, which had sufficient capacity to ensure five to six discharges of the flamethrower; a pump would have to refill the accumulator as quickly as possible. Rapid opening of the spray nozzle was considered important. Inside the nozzle there was a shutoff valve. This also had the advantage that no more flame oil could run after, which could serve as an easier target point for the enemy. To ensure reliable ignition of the jet, Wegmann used a very fine nozzle that was attached to a secondary line.

The resulting fine mist was ignited by a spark plug. For guaranteed ignition, two nozzles and two spark plugs were always available. The ignition spark was produced by an induction coil with buzzer and capacitor. For optimal range, the flame jet had to remain bundled for as long as possible; to achieve this required an exact interaction between initial velocity and nozzle diameter. Wegmann had amassed good experience in reducing range by reducing pressure, but only within small limits. Adjusting the spray head's elevation to regulate distance was seen as more effective. The table on page 158 shows the flamethrowers developed by Wegmann and their different ranges.

The last system was the most suitable variant. Krupp tasked *Diplom-Ingenieur* Bode of the Wegmann company to develop a piston pump that, using the existing pressure tanks, was to spray the flame oil with a pressure of 284 to 313 psi. Wegmann & Co. received a contract for the development and delivery of the flamethrower system, which was given the highest-priority level of DE 4818-0183/43. Installation of the spray head with a traverse of 180 degrees still had to be looked into, however. On September 16, 1943, the participants met again for talks. The schematic arrangement for a flamethrower system for a "larger" armored vehicle and the design of a double-piston pump were presented. This revealed that the double-piston pump would be powered by a pressure fluid from a pressure tank.

With each pump stroke, left and right, the outer piston forced flame oil through an activated external slider to the

Range	147–164'	195'	295'
Emission volume	1.6–1.85 gal./sec.	1.85–2.1 gal./sec.	4 gal./sec.
Pressure	185–200 psi	228 psi	284–313 psi
Nozzle diameter	0.5"	0.55"	0.70"
Pump power	22–25 hp	28 hp	90 hp
Initial velocity	190 fps	157 fps	196 fps

spray head. The manually activated control slider selectively released the piston pump for the left or right side. This piston pump was unusual, since centrifugal pumps were used in other flamethrowers. Engineer Bode had nothing against this arrangement in principle but intimated that because of the usual contamination of the flame oil in the form of tar, small pebbles, and acids, it must make the use of collars of any kind to seal the pistons impossible. Sealing the piston could be achieved only through the use of piston rings. Because of the serious contamination of the flame oil, the control elements were also to be easily accessible so that they could be cleaned at any time.

There were also experiments with particularly pure flame oil. *Wa Prüf* 5 had already conducted experiments with diesel as a flame medium, but they had not gone satisfactorily. There was another problem with the flame oil at temperatures lower than –13 degrees Fahrenheit. To be able to use the viscous flame oil at these temperatures, Wegmann envisaged heating the spray head. Engineer Bode thought it important that the pressure and speed of the flame jet be kept even. A loss of pressure in the hydraulic pressure tank from 1,990 to 1,710 psi resulted in a pressure drop from 327 to 285 psi in the flame oil jet. There followed the suggestion that the required 270 ft. range would require a relatively large quantity of flame oil. For comparison, Engineer Bode specified a quantity of 264 gallons of flame oil for a range of 164 ft. and a nozzle diameter of 0.55 inches. There followed the presentation of four flamethrower systems and designs from Wegmann & Co.:

1. The design of a jet tube in the machine gun mount of the *Panzerkampfwagen* III included a system with foot operation and a needle at the end of the spray head. This needle was also envisaged for the Krupp design.

2. The design of a spray head that was movable 8 degrees in azimuth and elevation. This design had since been abandoned, however, because the rubber hoses it used were subject to destruction for the reasons listed above.

3. The design for a spray head that was movable in azimuth and elevation. The primarily unbalanced spray head could be moved in elevation by means of a gear drive.

4. The design of a 295 ft. flamethrower system for the *Panzerkampfwagen Maus*. Adjustments in elevation could be achieved with the aid of pressure regulation. Horizontally, the small turret-like structure could rotate 180 degrees. Transmission of the rotation movements to the flame oil lines was accomplished by means of a connecting link. To calm the flow of flame oil before exiting the nozzle head, a slight bowing of 59 to 79 inches was envisaged.

While the design work had made significant progress, the preparation of the necessary materials was causing considerable problems. On May 6, 1943, Professor Dr. Müller, the director of Krupp, handed the complete raw-materials requirement for the *Urling* project to *Hauptdienstleiter* Karl-Otto Saur of the Reich Ministry of Armaments and Munitions. The detailed list included **50,750 tons of alloyed and unalloyed steel**, and another **336 tons of nonferrous metals, including 220 tons of copper alone**. For the planned five vehicles, this resulted in a materials requirement of **10,150 tons of alloyed and unalloyed steel** and about **44 tons of copper** for each vehicle, with the spare barrel and ammunition included in these quantities.

The left rotating 90 mm flamethrower on the wooden model of the *Maus* tank

For better comparison, examine the following figures:

- 207-ton *Maus* tank, required 308 tons of raw steel
- 76-ton *Tiger B*, 132 tons of raw steel (48.5 tons of unalloyed and 84 tons of alloyed steel)
- 49-ton *Panther D*, 86 tons of raw steel (37.5 tons of unalloyed and 48.5 tons of alloyed steel)
- 27.5-ton *Panzer* IV tank, 43 tons of raw steel[35]

Another example for the huge materials requirements of the *Urling* project is evident in a comparison with the raw-steel requirements for the ongoing monthly production of tanks by Krupp, which envisaged 14,991 tons of raw steel for production of all tank types in the mid-1943 period. Of the requested

quantity of 50,750 tons, the materials required for the third quarter of 1943, approximately 4,442 tons of steel and 22 tons of copper were to be readied as quickly as possible so that the assembly of the first device could begin.

On June 1, 1943, Dr. Weinwurm, the responsible representative for raw-materials allocation in the armaments office, informed Krupp that the written contract for the materials for production of the *Urling* had been signed by Armaments Minister Speer, whose written order with the contract number DE 4818-0183/43, the highest priority level, bore the date May 25, 1943. Then, on June 8, 1943, Krupp presented the submission for procurement of the MB 507 engines to *Hauptdienstleiter* Saur of the armaments office; however, as of August 1943 a decision had still not been

Time	Steel	Copper	Device 1	Device 2	Device 3	Device 4	Device 5	Barrels	Ammunition
3.Q.1943	4,029 t	19.845 t							
4.Q.1943	4,029 t	19.845 t							
1.Q.1944	4,029 t	19.845 t							
2.Q.1944	4,029 t	19.845 t							
3.Q.1944	4,029 t	19.42 t							
4.Q.1944	4,029 t	19.32 t							
1.Q.1945	4,029 t	19.3 t							
2.Q.1945	4,029 t	19.3 t							
3.Q.1945	4,029 t	19.3 t							
4.Q.1945	4,029 t	19.3 t							
1.Q.1946	1,820 t	0.965 t							
2.Q.1946		0.965 t							
3.Q.1946		0.965 t							
4.Q.1946		0.865 t							
1.Q.1947									
Total	46,040 t		9,208 t Steel	9,208 t Steel	9,208 t Steel	9,208 t Steel	9,208 t Steel		
		Is 199 t	40 t Copper	40 t Copper	40 t Copper	40 t Copper	40 t Copper		

made. *Hauptamtsleiter* Saur therefore had to energetically remind Daimler-Benz several times to produce a delivery plan for the planned diesel engines.

On September 21, 1943, Daimler-Benz's response concerning the delivery of forty-four examples of the MB 507 diesel engine reached the Reich Ministry for Armaments and Munitions. In it, Daimler-Benz advised that production of the forty-four MB 507 engines (five vehicles + four spare engines) for the *Veilchen* device, in addition to the existing marine production capacity, could begin in April 1944, with four MB 507s per month. First, however, the following conditions had to be met:

1. Procurement of raw materials with the highest priority:
■ the large cast parts by December 1943
■ externally produced parts, such as the crankshafts, by February 1944

2. Machinery and installations:
■ soonest allocation of two long-called-for universal fast-turning lathes

3. Accelerated completion of technical devices already ordered:
■ by December 1943 at the latest

4. Allocation of thirty-five workers, at least one-third of them German workers:
■ twenty-eight machinists and seven metalworkers
■ monthly allocation of an additional twelve fitters from December 1943 onward

Krupp produced the first detailed plans for production sequences on September 28, 1943. Dr. Müller based his figures on the production of five devices.

For production of the guns, this meant that orders for forgings would have to be placed by October 1, 1943, since it was estimated that about fourteen months would be required to finish the barrels. The first barrel would thus be completed sometime after December 1, 1944. Dr. Müller no longer thought that special tests for the gun's internal ballistics would be required:

	Barrel Complete	Device Ready for Collection	Spare Barrel Liner Complete
1st Device	December 1, 1944	January 1, 1945	April 1, 1946
2nd Device	April 1, 1945	May 1, 1945	July 1, 1946
3rd Device	July 1, 1945	August 1, 1945	October 1, 1946
4th Device	October 1, 1945	November 1, 1945	January 1, 1947
5th Device	January 1, 1946	February 1, 1946	April 1, 1947

1. To meet the target date for completion of the first device, the contract for the gun cradle would have to be issued immediately.
2. It was assumed that five months of procurement time for the cast parts, followed by seven months of production time, would be required for the elevating and traversing mechanism.
3. Design of the loader, however, could not yet be completed.
4. The ordering of engines from Daimler-Benz could happen only with the help of the Ministry of Armaments and Munitions.
5. The electrical systems had been theoretically clarified with Siemens-Schuckert, but as of yet no schedule had been worked out.
6. Ordering of the necessary cooling system could take place in the near future.
7. The readying of armor sheet was seen as possible; however, it remained to be determined whether capacity permitted this in addition to other tank production.
8. The sheet metal, initially for the lower parts, could be provided in fourteen days, and for the upper parts in about six weeks.
9. Krupp had planned the installation of the planned mine-clearing equipment on the vehicle in such a way that the subsequent installation should not be a problem if required.
10. The necessary ammunition cars were in part to be produced by Krupp itself, and in part purchased from the Reichsbahn.

For the necessary ammunition vehicles, the use of the ammunition transporter for the *Karl* heavy howitzer, based on the *Panzerkampfwagen* IV, might be possible. For rail transport of the *Urling* armored howitzer, which would be broken down into eight sections, Krupp envisaged the following cars per device:

- eight heavy freight cars of unknown type for the equipment sections
- three SSI cars (four-axle rail cars with 18-meter load length) for the crane
- three Rs cars (stake cars) for the crane
- two Rs cars for the accessories
- two Glt cars (covered, large-capacity freight cars with front doors) for the accessories
- one Glt car for the workshop
- an undetermined number of cars for the necessary operating crew

Krupp estimated that a total of 5,000 rounds of ammunition would have to be produced for each gun. It took as a basis a barrel life of 500 rounds. The requirement per gun in detail:

- 100 concrete shells
- 200 explosive shells
- 200 mine shells

For five planned devices plus one spare barrel liner each, this resulted in a total requirement for 1,000 concrete shells, 2,000 explosive shells, and 2,000 mine shells. Manufacture of the concrete and mine shells was to take place at Krupp. Dr. Müller was able to envisage the bringing in of outside companies for the production of the explosive shells, and he also anticipated a production period of twenty-seven months, beginning in October 1944 and continuing until about the end of 1946. This meant an average monthly production of 185 shells. Concerning production of casings, which were to be the easier-to-produce wrapped type, initial negotiations with the Polte Company had already begun.

On October 7, 1943, there was another meeting at Krupp in Essen on the subject of the "Urling deadlines." Those responsible calculated that the five devices would be delivered at six-month intervals; each device required about fourteen months of work for completion. As a condition, the participating gentlemen felt that this could be achieved provided the armaments ministry provided sufficient work forces and workshop services. For the area of the vehicle workshop, Dr. Müller estimated about 100,000 to 120,000 wage hours per device, which meant an additional requirement for about 100 workers. By comparison, it should be noted that an average of about 2,000 hours was required to complete a Panzerkampfwagen V Panther.

As further conditions for production of the Urling, Krupp would have to rebuild Factory Hall No. 1 (internally designated "Ship 1") and Factory Hall No. 2, which had been destroyed by Allied bombing, within two months. Furthermore, Workshop Hall 4 would have to be completely available for Urling production. Furthermore, Director Dr. Müller calculated 16,000 to 17,000 pay hours for workshop areas 9/10, which meant an additional personnel requirement of about seventy workers.

The participants proposed bringing in the necessary personnel from the Italian prisoner-of-war camps or from industry. In addition, existing armaments contracts had to be taken into consideration in planning the Urling project. The carriage workshop, for example, was required to produce one K-3 or one Siegfried Gerät railroad gun every five months. Those responsible also had to take into consideration the contract that envisaged completion of the R-2, a tracked 280 mm gun, by the first half of 1944.

The contents of the next statement, made at the conclusion of the meeting, were so striking that they will be repeated here:

Since completion of the first Urling cannot be expected before the end of 1945 and by that time will probably no longer be of interest, perhaps will even be overtaken by simpler and lighter devices, and since the development work in the Eugen and Burger groups still requires about 1,200 design hours, which can be achieved by these groups only if all other tasks are abandoned, it must be considered whether the Urling should not be completely deferred and other ancillary devices be produced instead. The late delivery deadline is mainly attributable to a shortage of labor forces. Urling shall not be stopped in the interim, but for the time being no further parts shall be assigned.

Consideration should be given to replacing the Urling with a larger-caliber device (52 or possibly 60) for R projectiles, to be installed on the Tiger in a similar way as the 580 mm projector by Alkett. Firing range would have to be at least 2.5, or, better, 3 miles, and the projectiles should contain 880, or, better, 1,100 lbs. of explosives. Another meeting on this topic will take place in eight days."[36]

This statement reflects very well the reality in the German armaments companies at that time and possesses the character of a final stroke on the subject of the Urling.

Neither material allocations nor an answer from Hauptdienstleiter Saur, the responsible department head in the ministry for armaments and munitions, followed by the end of October. On November 12, 1943, Krupp made a proposal to the armaments representative that if a third of the raw materials could not be made available immediately, that it would suffice if at least the material for one device could be made available for the fourth quarter of 1943. Krupp gave as further possible deadlines concerning the necessary materials allocations the third and fourth quarters of 1944, the first and third quarters of 1945, and the first quarter of 1946. On January 29, 1944, Daimler-Benz received a letter from Krupp stating that for particular reasons, the execution of the contract for 44 MB 507 diesel engines had been deferred. The ultimate end of the Urling project came on December 22, 1944, in a letter from Krupp to Herr Hölkeskamp of the armaments agency, which read: "Since it is at present impossible to say when, because of conditions here, the above project [Urling] can begin, we submit the enclosed retransfer no. 1/01/E of 21/12/1943 concerning 2,524 tons of unalloyed and 1,907 tons of alloyed steel with the request that this be forwarded to Herr Dr. Weinwurm of the R.f.R.u.M."[37]

Mention of the canceled Urling project was made, however, at a later date, on March 1, 1944. A license contract for the Escher-Wyas gas turbine, in which the Krupp AK department had great interest, was mentioned in several letters between Dr. Müller and Professor K. von Sanden of the Krupp-Germaniawerft AG. Professor Sanden thanked Dr. Müller for his support in procuring this license for a gas turbine and asked if Krupp still had interest in a high-performance power system of about 10,000 hp. Dr. Müller wrote back: "Although the intended purpose no longer exists at AK, since we have meanwhile had to help others, we continue to have great interest in such a principle, even if only intellectually."[38]

On June 15, 1944, a meeting was held between representatives of the Germaniawerft and Krupp AK in Essen on the topic of combustion turbines. Referring to the drawings of the *Urling*, they discussed the space, weight, propulsion, and performance conditions in AK devices. It was considered necessary to install a turbine capable of producing 10,000 hp in the space needed for a 6,400 hp diesel system with no increase in weight. The release of gases from the exhaust was to be temporarily possible underwater with a counter-pressure of a 13 ft. (4 m) column of water. Since combustion turbines usually reacted very slowly to sudden power increases, the gas turbine was to enable a fast-acting power regulation during the sudden power changes typically encountered in land vehicles. However, this led to a worsening of the degree of effectiveness, which due to increased fuel consumption resulted in reduced range. The difficult delivery and discharge of the required large quantities of cooling air were also seen as problematic in a large armored vehicle. Development work on the Escher-Wyss gas turbine by the Germaniawerft therefore remained limited to use as ship propulsion units.

Technical Overview of the Large Tank Project Designs:

	P-1000 Grote	800 mm Armored Howitzer	600 mm Armored Howitzer	*Urling*
Gross weight	800–1,000 tons	1,794 tons (without mine)	801 tons	1,049
Gun weight	300 tons	total 297 tons	total 167 tons	
Barrel		149 tons	90 tons	81 tons
Cradle		65 tons	50 tons	
Bearing end shield		6 tons	5 tons	
Ammunition lifts		10 tons	7 tons	
Loader		7 tons	5 tons	
Elevation mechanism		10 tons	10 tons	
Flak turret	deleted	30 tons	deleted	
Flamethrower	deleted	20 tons	deleted	
Armor	200 tons	645 tons	284 tons	
Iron construction	200 tons	492 tons	178 tons	
Running gear (with motors)	100 tons	310 tons	132 tons	
Machinery	100 tons	50 tons	40 tons	
Length	111/115'	83.6'	72'	72.6'
Width	33/46'	42'	29'	34'
Height	36'	27'	23'	23'
Firing height	unknown	20.6'	17'	17'
Armament:				
Main armament	two 305 mm SK/ 280 mm SK	800 mm howitzer	600 mm howitzer	600 mm howitzer
Barrel length		L/13.6 = 35.6'	L/21 = 40.35'	L/20.5 = 39'
Recoil and recoil length		2,000 tons and 6.5'	1,000 tons and 4.9'	1,300 tons and 4.9'

Other armament	four 150 mm K/ 128 mm K	flak turret		two flamethrowers for 295'
Close defense	eight 20 mm MG 151	flamethrower		10 times M.G. stands
Armor:				
Front	11.8"	9.85"	9.85"	5.9/7.9"
Side upper/lower	9.85"	3.9/5.9"	3.9/4.7"	3.9"
Rear		3.9"	3.9"	3.9"
Roof	3"	7.9"	7.9"	5.9/7"
Floor (front/back)	3.9"	5.9/2/1"	5.9/2/1"	
Power plants	12 MB 501 with 2,000 hp	4 MB 501 with 2,000 hp	4 MB 502 with 1,350 hp	8 MB 507 with 800 hp
Output	64,000 hp at 1,650 rpm	8,000 hp at 1,630 rpm	5,400 hp at 1,650 rpm	6,400 hp at 2,200 rpm
Power transfer	hydraulic			electric
Power-to-weight ratio	64 hp/ton	4.46 hp/ton	6.74 hp/ton	6.1 hp/ton
Speed	25 mph	4.3 mph	5 mph	6.2 mph
Ground pressure	11.4 psi / 7.6 psi	21 psi	23 psi	26 psi
Track contact surface	65–69'	42.6' = 1,291 ft.^{2}	34' = 532 ft.^{2}	34.8'
Track width	6 × 3.3/3.9'	8 × 3.3'	4 × 3.6'	4 × 3.85'
Track		25.5'	19'	19.8'
Steering ratio		1.65	1.8	1.76
Running gear	road wheels D = 6.5'	128 double rollers		128 double rollers with D = 20.8"
Suspension	hydropneumatic			compressed air with spring deviation of 15.75"
Trench-crossing ability				16.5'
Ground clearance	6.6'			
Fording ability	26.25'			19.7'
Climbing ability	15.75'			2.8'
Max. climb angle	30°			30°
Types of ammunition		concrete/H.E./ howitzer shells	concrete shell	concrete/H.E./ howitzer shells
Projectile weight		15,432/10,582/13,277 lbs.	6,613 lbs.	6,613/5,291/5,291 lbs.
Initial velocity (fps)		1,148/1,394/492	1,263/1,279	1,345/1,476/1,476
Normal pressure (psi)		34,146/1,394/21,335	21,335	28,446/23,752/1,394
Barrel elevation		0 to 70°	0 to 70°	0 to 70°
Muzzle energy		44,000 mt /1,394/6,900 mt	23,300 mt	26,300 mt / 25,300 mt
Maximum firing range (miles)		6.8/9.3/1.35	8.7	9/9.8/9
Ammunition capacity				8 rounds in magazine
Crew	40 men			

Appendix

The *Heereswaffenamt* (Army Ordnance Office) between 1940 and 1944

The purpose of this chapter is to clarify the connections between the work of the Army Ordnance Office, so often described in this book, and its *Amtsgruppen*, as well as the committees and special plenipotentiaries employed by the Armaments Ministry (*Rm.d.B.u.M.*, and, from autumn 1943, *Rm.f.R.u.K.*). The state and the party exerted a growing influence as the war went on. The minister for armaments and munitions increasingly took over the former functions and areas of responsibility of the army. In doing so, he attempted to achieve an optimized concentration and focus on the state's war potential. Organizationally, the following were created for the individual weapons categories, munitions, and vehicles:

- committees "for development"
- boards for "mass production"
- pools "for the manufacture of semifinished products"

These belonged to the respective representatives of industry and the military. In his position as commander in chief of the *Wehrmacht*, Adolf Hitler exerted a growing influence on major decisions as to the introduction or rejection of new weapons.

Normally, the monthly output requirements and the approval for new weapons, equipment, and ammunition came from the General Army Office (AHA) and its Weapons Inspectorates (In). The Army Ordnance Office (HWA) was responsible for the technical design and production of new weapons, equipment, and munitions. In the named period the HWA was under the chief of army mobilization and the commander of the home army (Chef H.Rüst. u. B.d.E.)—namely, *Generaloberst* Fromm—and after June 20, 1944, the *Reichsführer-SS* Himmler. In detail, the responsibilities of the HWA, as of 1940 led by *General der Artillerie* Emil Leeb were the following:

- development of new weapons, equipment, and munitions by the Development and Testing Group (*Wa Prüf*)
- mass procurement of weapons, equipment, and munitions by the Group for Weapons and Equipment Manufacture (*Wa I Rü WuG*) and Munitions (*Wa I Rü Mun*)
- preparation for mass production by industry and the technical foundation for it by the Chief Engineer Group (*Wa Chef Ing*)
- acceptance of completed weapons, equipment, and munitions by the Acceptance Group (*Wa Abn*)
- Central Group of Army Ordnance Office (*Wa Z*) was responsible for all tasks of an economic or organizational nature necessary for the guidance and processing of the office's entire area.

In addition, as well as a headquarters (*Wa Stab*) there was a research department (*Wa F*), whose responsibilities included liaising with the other research facilities of the Reich as well as basic and applied research. The HWA attached the *Wa Prüf* to this department as of 1944. Because of the developments specially treated in this book, the Development and Testing Group takes center place in the description. In 1943, the OKH named as its chief *Generalleutnant* Erich Schneider, who had previously exercised the functions of *Chef Wa Prüf* 1 and *Chef Wa Prüf* 4. In between, he carried out command functions at the front.

At that time the group consisted of twelve *Abteilungen* (departments):

- *Abteilung Prüf* 1, Ballistics and Munitions, which was organized into four groups on the basis of type of weapon:
  — Infantry Group
  — Antitank Group
  — Division Artillery Group
  — Corps and Army Artillery
  as well as nine other groups for munitions and ballistics (including at Kummersdorf)

- *Abteilung Prüf* 2, infantry with small-caliber weapons up to 20 mm (locations included Kummersdorf)
- *Abteilung Prüf* 4, artillery with large-caliber weapons from 20 mm and upward, which were organized into eight groups depending on type of gun (locations included Hillersleben and Rügenwalde)
- *Abteilung Prüf* 5, mines and engineer equipment (locations included Sperenberg-Klausdorf)
- *Abteilung Prüf* 6, tanks and motorization, chief was *Oberstleutnant* Philipps until 1937; from 1937 to 1942, *Oberstleutnant* Fichtner, and from 1942 onward, *Oberstleutnant* Holzhäuer

The department was divided into the

  — Headquarters Group under *Oberstleutnant* Wollenhaupt
  — Main Group Tank under *Oberst* Crohn
  — Main Group Motorization under *Hauptmann* Winterfeld
  — Main Group Research under *Ministerialrat* Kniepkamp (locations included Kummersdorf, Berkam Tripoli in Libya, Roeris in Norway, and St. Johann in Tyrol)

- *Abteilung Prüf* 7, signals equipment, organized into the headquarters group and seven other groups
- *Abteilung Prüf* 8, optics, observation, and measuring equipment, organized in five groups
- *Abteilung Prüf* 9, gas defense, smoke, and warfare agents (location in Spandau)
- *Abteilung Prüf Festungs-Pioniere, Befestigungswesen*, fortress engineers and fortifications
- *Abteilung Prüf* 11, rockets and special devices (locations included Kummersdorf and Peenemünde)
- *Abteilung Prüf* 12, experimental stations, organized into five groups

The Army Ordnance Office's personnel consisted of officers with technical-college training, officers with moderate technical training, and civilian officials and employees. There were also auxiliary personnel for office and other duties, as well as guard and duty personnel. The first-named officers alternated between service at the front and activity in the office and accounted for the majority of the advisors and department heads in the *Wa Prüf*. The officers with moderate technical training were the specialists or were often active in acceptance, frequently including officers from the firefighting service. The senior and midlevel technical officials supplemented the employees and represented the responsible cadre during the constant changing of officers in the office. This can be seen in the example of *Wa Prüf* 6, where three *Amtsgruppen* chiefs had to work their way in within a relatively short time, while Ernst Kniepkamp, who had been active in his office for almost twenty years and was the recognized expert and group leader, was not fooled by anything. In the years from 1941 to 1944, the HWA's personnel strength, after compulsory cuts, was about 5,000 to 6,000 men, and that of the test facilities was about 2,000 men.[39]

Brief Biographies

Ernst Kniepkamp

Dipl.Ing. Heinrich Ernst Kniepkamp was born in Wuppertal on January 5, 1895. After the First World War he studied at the Karlsruhe Technical College. He subsequently worked for MAN as a transmission designer and later joined an engineering company in Rostock for a short time. In 1926, he moved to the *Heereswaffenamt Berlin*. His area of responsibility was mainly planning and development of wheeled, half-tracked, and tracked carriages. Despite limited resources, in 1930–31 Kniepkamp created the first stationary test stand for tracked vehicles at the *Verskraft (alt)* (experimental station for old motor vehicles). In 1932–33, together with his first associate in the Research Group, Engineer Franke, he worked out the basis for the future half-tracked tractors and armored vehicles of the *Wehrmacht*. During that time, he worked closely with Karl Maybach, whose company produced the engines for the tracked-vehicle project by Kniepkamp. Through this close relationship with Maybach-Motorenbau, he laid the foundations for the compact six- and twelve-cylinder gasoline engines that powered German tracked vehicles.

After joining the development department of *Wa Prüf* 6 at the end of 1936, Kniepkamp planned a standardization of the running gear and transmissions of the *Panzer* III and IV, during which he also worked on marketing his patents. This often placed him in conflicts of interest with the major tank manufacturers, such as Krupp and Daimler-Benz, which operated their own research and development divisions. Consequently, Kniepkamp favored companies such as Henschel, MAN, and Famo in awarding contracts, which he could control through his influence on the *Amtsgruppen* heads *Oberst* Phillip, *Oberst* Fichtner, and *Oberst* Holzhäuer.

Despite his efforts to achieve standardization in German tank construction, he had to endure harsh criticism from Krupp. This was due mainly to his technically complex and costly interleaved suspension, which he took directly from half-tracked prime movers. Other suspension and transmission designs, such as the Variorex transmission by Maybach, which Kniepkamp had installed, led to considerable modification work on the *Panzer* III by manufacturers Krupp and Daimler-Benz. At MAN, too, leading designers had to design contrary to their convictions to follow Kniepkamp's wishes, so that in the example of the *Las* 100 the design had to be completely changed repeatedly. As a result, in 1939 the responsibility for decisions concerning guidelines for tanks passed to *Oberstleutnant* Olbrich.

Until the end of the war, *Ministerialrat* Kniepkamp worked in the *Heereswaffenamt* as head of Main Group F (Research) in *Amtsgruppe Wa Prüf* 6. The seat of his office was in the *neuen Verskraft* (new experimental station for motor vehicles) at the Kummersdorf Artillery Range, Building 11. Despite all the criticism, he was an outstanding engineer and had about fifty patents in the field of tracked vehicles. After the war he established an engineering office, where he worked in his favored field of tracked vehicles.[40]

Karl-Otto Saur

Karl-Otto Saur was born in Düsseldorf on February 16, 1902. After attending primary and secondary school in Freiburg until 1926, he studied business studies and mechanical engineering at the University of Freiburg and the technical colleges in Karlsruhe and Hanover. He subsequently joined August-Thyssen-Hütte in Duisburg as an engineer, where he was responsible for the automation of work processes. In 1929, he took over his father's steel construction business. After this company went bankrupt, in October 1930 he returned to Thyssen and beginning in 1932 headed the company's business administration department as senior engineer.

In 1931, he took part in a study trip to the Soviet Union, which was developing technically, and he was very impressed by its industry and its centralized leadership. After joining the NSDAP in 1931, in 1935 he became District Office head of technology in Essen, where among other things he set up a file system to record data on all German engineers. In 1939, Saur functioned as Fritz Todt's chief of staff and deputy in the Nazi Party's main office for technology. In 1940, he moved to the Ministry of Armaments and Munitions under Speer. Starting in February 1942, he headed the ministry's *Technische Amt* (technical office), and in September 1943 he was made responsible for the production of all armaments for the *Wehrmacht*. In August 1944, Hitler named him chief of staff of the so-called fighter staff and in 1945 named him Speer's successor in his will.[41] After he was arrested in 1945, he served as a witness for the prosecution at the Nuremberg trials. As a result he was regarded as a camp follower and, socially isolated, was discharged in 1948.

Erich Müller

Born in Berlin on November 2, 1892, Müller studied at the Berlin Technical College from 1919 until 1922. After graduating as an engineer, he worked briefly as a designer in the Borsig-Werken, subsequently serving as assistant at the TH Berlin until the end of 1922. In 1931 he achieved his doctorate in engineering, and in 1934 he became director of the RAW Berlin-Tempelhof. He began his career with Krupp AG in 1935 and a year later became head of the artillery development division, where he played a major role in the development of twenty-four gun types, achieving a major milestone in weapons technology with the development of the *Dora* 800 mm gun. This earned him the nickname "cannon Müller."

In 1938 he assumed the position of deputy director, and in 1940 he was named head of the weapons committee in the War Ministry. In the spring of 1942, he left the committee as the result of differences with Todt and Speer. Hitler named him professor on January 30, 1943. After the end of 1943, he dedicated himself exclusively to the development of weapons, especially artillery designs. At the Nuremberg trials in 1945, he was sentenced to twelve years' imprisonment, in large part due to statements made by Saur.

Edward F. Grote

Unfortunately, not much is known about this designer. In 1929–30, *Dipl.Ing.* Edward Grote and his design bureau were invited to the Soviet Union to help build up mechanical engineering in the country. In Leningrad in 1930, he began development work on a heavily armored medium tank. After several, partially unsuccessful designs, in 1933 Grote had to leave the Soviet Union. In Germany he worked in the newly created Armaments Ministry. During the war, Speer, in his capacity as the Third Reich's minister for armaments and munitions, named Grote special plenipotentiary for submarine construction. Grote's trail disappeared after the war in South Africa, where on April 28, 1950, he applied for a patent in the GDR.

Fallacies

In addition to the technical questionability of the project, the above-mentioned article from the German military periodical *Die Kraftfahrkampfgruppe*, issue 9/1937, raises questions as to why an article on Edward Grote's work in the Soviet Union was published. It does seem quite likely that Grote had important information about Soviet armaments. In retrospect, however, it looks as though it was intentional disinformation on the part of the Soviet intelligence service, which appears to have succeeded. From the German side, this publication was probably intended to unsettle the population concerning the threat from the east, adding another argument in favor of the then-growing rearmament of Germany.

A Russian 1,000-Ton Tank?

In the late 1930s, a heavily illustrated article about a 1,000-ton tank, supposedly designed for Soviet Russia by a German mechanical engineer between 1930 and 1934, appeared in a widely read German periodical. In addition to the pictures, one of which shows the tank serving as a coastal battery in combat with warships, the article also contains a drawing of the basic design and the following specification:

- general dimensions: length, 111.5 feet; width, 36 feet
- armament: two 305 mm and four 150 mm cannon in twin-gun turrets, as well as smaller-caliber guns
- armor: forward, 11.8 inches; sides, 9.8 inches; bottom, 3.93 inches; top, 3 inches
- propulsion system: 24,000 hp
- speed: 31 mph

This report seems so fantastic and unbelievable that it stimulates a few calculations to verify it, but they are so simple that any clever fifteen-year-old can check them. There are surprising results:

1. The ground pressure of a tracked vehicle must be only about a third of a kilogram for each square centimeter to prevent sinking. Because this tank weighs 1,000,000 kilograms, it must rest on 3,000,000 cm²; that is, 300 square meters. However, the entire undersurface of the tank is roughly that large. The tracks must therefore take up the entire width of the tank. This is contradicted not only by the illustrations, but also because it makes turning unthinkable. In the majority of tanks

Ein ruffifcher Taufend-Tonnen-Tank.

created to date, the tracks account for approximately one-fourth of the total width of the vehicle. For these dimensions, this 1,000-ton tank is four times too heavy!

2. The weight of the main armor can be figured out roughly from the main dimensions listed above and the armor thicknesses, while a height of about 20 feet can be estimated from the pictures. This gives a weight of more than 2,200 tons, which is twice the weight of the entire vehicle!

3. On the basis of the drawing and the illustrations, the engine compartment can be only 26 feet long and wide and about 15 feet deep. It seems impossible that it could accommodate a 24,000 hp propulsion system with fuel tanks. A propulsion system that powerful would require a space that is at least as large as the entire vehicle!

4. On the basis of the design drawing, the 305 mm gun is approximately 30 feet long. However, full-fledged guns of that caliber have a length of approximately 55 feet. Therefore something isn't right!

5. The speed of the vehicle is given as 30 miles per hour. Experience has shown, however, that increasing the size and weight of a tank inevitably reduces its speed. While the new light tanks are capable of speeds of 30 miles per hour, the French 77- and 99-ton heavy tanks are capable of only 7.5 miles per hour. The driving speed of a 1,100-ton tank can therefore be estimated at 3 miles per hour at best, 10 percent of the claimed value.

6. Finally, there are other technical problems that will be almost impossible to resolve, such as, for example, the road wheel suspension. With regard to "sucking" obstacles, the suspension must have a vertically sprung freedom of movement of precisely 1 meter. How will this be achieved with such weights?

From a military standpoint it should be mentioned that such large-caliber guns are viable only for engaging important targets far behind the enemy's front. In a major war this can be achieved by both sides with much-simpler and therefore less expensive means. The most significant of these guns is the famous German cannon that shelled Paris. With the use of modern bombing aircraft, however, this type of gun is scarcely worth considering.

But the monstrosity of a 1,100-ton tank is also too expensive as a coastal battery. Modern targeting systems allow coastal guns to be placed under cover, making it possible to do without the expensive tank.

One therefore comes to the unquestionable conclusion that this design is unfeasible from a technical point of view, but also impractical from a tactical viewpoint. The question now arises of whether it is right to unsettle the readers of a popular periodical with reports of a huge but, in reality, impractical weapon of war from a state that is hostile toward Germany. Soviet Russia's huge rearmament program is still growing, so that this fact alone is sufficient to strain the will to defend Germany to the utmost. It is very wrong, however, to invent stories about gigantic enemy weapons of war, which to the layman seem unbeatable.

Generalbaurat d. R. Ing. Günther Burstyn

The designer of the 1,100-ton tank, Edward Grote, commented as follows:

In 1929, the Russians signed me to a contract, initially to put my specialized knowledge and years of experience in building vehicles and

Ein russischer Tausend=Tonnen=Tank.

engines at the disposal of Soviet industry. Then, following my arrival in Moscow, I was, without special formalities, given the task of applying this knowledge in the field of armaments. During this time, encouraged by my successful work in Soviet-Russian armaments factories, I had the opportunity on a number of occasions to personally discuss the problems associated with motorization in depth with Deputy Commissar of War Tukhachevsky, and in doing so gain a deep insight into his thought processes and the wishes of his counterparts in this field. After the 27.5-ton and 33-ton medium tanks designed by me had met all the requirements, Tukhachevsky and his staff gave me the task of designing a 110-ton breakthrough tank similar to the French char de rupture D 2. The requirements for this machine were extraordinarily difficult, and there were several times when the assigned tasks seemed impossible. The ultimately successful construction proved, however, that with sufficient experience and more thorough knowledge of the subject, even problems that at first seemed fantastic could be mastered to the extent that the reality left from this fantasy was astonishing. Capable engineering personnel played a major role in the work.

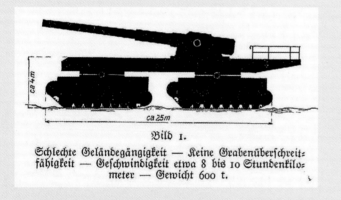

Bild 1.

Schlechte Geländegängigkeit — Keine Grabenüberschreit-fähigkeit — Geschwindigkeit etwa 8 bis 10 Stundenkilo-meter — Gewicht 600 t.

While preparations for construction of the 110-ton tank were in progress, discussions about the design of a "fortress tank" began, with the justification that the frontiers of Soviet-Russian territory were so vast that fortifications after the European example (France) were out of the question and that new ways and new means had to be sought and found. One of the officers in Tukhachevksy's circle declared: "In the world war you Germans shocked your opponents with your long-range guns; why should you not able to also achieve above the average in tank design?" Although I was of course not deserving of such praise, it did not fail to have the effect of spurring me to approach my task with all energy. The experience and test results gained with early tank types were extremely valuable, and it was these results in particular, some of which contradicted previous experience in tank design, that caused me to raise objections to *Herr* Burstyn's criticism of my information on the 1,100-ton tank project.

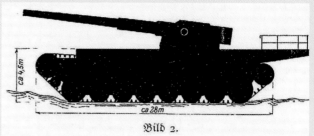

Bild 2.

Geländegängig — Gute taktische Eigenschaften — Angriffswaff mit Panzerschutz des Fahrwerkes und der Maschinenanlage — Geschwindigkeit etwa 25 Stundenkilometer — Gewicht 600 t

The weight of the mammoth vehicle was restricted to 1,100 tons. The silhouette images show how the train of thought developed. The Soviet-Russian military initially demanded an armament that included heavy artillery, so that the vehicle could take over the defense of frontiers and coasts from fixed fortifications. In addition, a "no-man's land belt" 2 to 3 miles deep was to be established along Russia's borders, in which these mobile fortresses were supposed to operate. The Russian terrain is very well suited to such a demand. There are few roads of the kind found in western Europe, and the same is true of bridges, apart from railroad bridges, which barely meet modern requirements and are often hundreds of miles apart. Even the 110-ton breakthrough tank caused problems in this regard, which is why consideration was given to improving the tank's fording capabilities. The 110-ton tank was 39 feet long and 10.5 feet wide and had a height of 9.3 feet. However, a fording depth of 12 feet was the minimum if the vehicle was to be capable of fording medium-size rivers in the country. The 1,100-ton tank could easily handle this fording depth.

The silhouette images show that the original thinking envisaged a vehicle whose nature was to be roughly equivalent to the familiar railway gun carriages. Its limited off-road capability resulted in the design not being pursued; however, the second proposal, to use

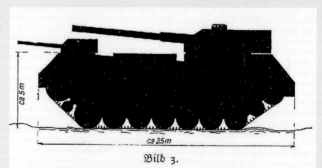

Bild 3.

Gute Geländegängigkeit — Gute taktische Eigenschaften — Voller Panzerschutz — Geschwindigkeit etwa 15 Stunden-kilometer — Als Sicherung hinter großen Truppen-verbänden — Gewicht etwa 900 bis 1000 t.

an enclosed self-propelled carriage, came closer to meeting the demands set. Its limited armor protection and low speed did not please the Russians, however. They placed great value in good armor protection as well as in high speed. From these considerations emerged a design similar to the third image. Once again, however, demands were raised so that the development envisaged a vehicle that, as can be seen from the perspective illustrations, was 111 ft. long, about 36 ft. high, and 32 ft. wide; had 6.5 ft. of ground clearance; and had up to 11.8 inches of armor in threatened locations, antiaircraft guns, and no ground defense, since a threat from field artillery was as good as excluded.

The propulsion system of this vehicle, the design of the running gear, and the suspension and the tracks were each a series of difficult problems that required months of consideration and review by sober minds, even before the notion of practicability could be embraced.

I would like to emphasize that to my knowledge, the 1,100-ton tank remains a "project" only to this day. But even in detail there is no agreement with the real design that came about in the course of development gained from other types and experience; rather, the descriptions depict only the thought processes seen in the war commissariat in Moscow years ago, on which basis Tukhachevsky gave me the task of considering and working out the project. The information reflects the military requirements of the Bolshevik marshals; the illustrations depict the first form of the theoretical constructs of that time, which in its monstrous impression does not fail to make Europe aware of what is going on in secret in the unimaginably vast spaces of Soviet Russia beyond the frontier trenches. May much that makes its way over from there remain utopia and fantasy. It was this threat that moved me to go public with this Soviet project for a 1,100-ton tank. I must vigorously reject the insinuations by Baurat Burstyn that I have made sensational claims to make the civilization of Europe nervous. I am familiar with *Herr* Burstyn's earlier work in the field of tanks, and I would never have expected the deviant position he has taken. But it requires more than an average ability to understand, which is obviously lacking, and first I will compare the forerunners of the 1,100-ton tank: the TG-1 (27.5 tons), TG-3 (33 tons), and the TG-5/T-42 (110 tons).

The TG-1/TG-3 Tanks

The ground pressure of the TG-1/T-22 medium tank (27.5 tons) built by me was 0.58 kg/cm², and that of the TG-3/T-29 (30 tons) was 8.5 psi. These vehicles were tested in the swamps near Leningrad and had a lower sink depth than the well-known Soviet-Russian T-18 light tank, an improved version of the French Renault. The same tank was wrongly identified as the S I and MS II in Fritz Heigl's *Taschenbuch der Tanks* ("Pocketbook of tanks"). The sink depth also depended on shape of the tracks.

Both machines had a speed of 27 miles per hour in meadow terrain. They drove in the swamps at 12 mph, and the sink depth was on average 3.9 to 5.9 inches, while the T-18 was already sliding on its belly over the reeds and thus sank deeper under the same operating conditions.

The TG-5/T-42 110-Ton Breakthrough Tank

On the basis of these results, I then built the TG-5/T-42 110-ton breakthrough tank, a counterpart to the French char de rupture.

The "100-ton tank" had a specific ground pressure of 9.24 psi. The vehicle had a width of 126 inches, a height of 112 inches, and an overall length of about 420 inches. Each track was 31.5 inches wide. The sixteen-cylinder engine developed 1,400 hp and, with supercharger, 1,800 hp for short periods. The tracks were driven by two special transmissions, each with a maximum performance of 1,000 hp; each transmission had 2 × 4 forward and reverse gears. A special 150 hp diesel engine delivered 75,000 cubic meters (cbm) of air through the radiator, which was necessary if the requirement for maintaining a coolant temperature of 194° F inside the engine with an outside temperature of 86° F was to be met. Armament consisted of one 105 mm gun in the main turret and two 37 mm defensive cannon, one in each of two revolving turrets, each with a coaxial machine gun. Two turrets in the rear of the tank each mounted a double machine gun for antiaircraft defense. Armor in the principal places was 3 inches. The machine easily ran at 25 mph and was child's play to operate, first with push button controls and later with a joystick similar to those used in aircraft. The command compartment in the very front was completely separated from the artillery compartment and was accessible by bulkhead doors similar to those in warships. Next to the driver sat the onboard mechanic. Transmission of commands from the command compartment in the main turret was by telephone, and radio equipment and a compass were envisaged. The tank had gas protection systems, whose effectiveness was never fully tested, however.

The running gear was—based on the good experience with the 33-ton tank—of similar design; however, the mechanical suspension was replaced by a hydraulic system, whose weight was almost half that of the mechanical system. Suspension effectiveness could be adjusted, and experiments in different terrain conditions to achieve the best accuracy by providing a stable firing platform while on the move were carried pout successfully. The Soviet Russians were understandably very pleased with the entire design and made great efforts to keep it secret.

The 1,100-Ton Tank

At the beginning of my statements I mentioned that at the same time that I was given the job of building the "100-ton breakthrough tank," which was designated the T-42, the war commissar also directed me to begin thinking about the structural design of the "fortress tank." Numerous designs were subsequently completed on the basis of the design and operating experience gained with the machines designed by me. There was nothing comparable, since all previous tanks were of much-lower performance. New guidelines for operating and tactical conditions had therefore been issued. The military requirements were issued by the war commissariat, and Tukhachevsky discussed them with me in great detail. At one of our meetings, he said this to me:

"Fortress works, such as those built by the European capitalist-bourgeois states, are not possible for securing the frontiers of the vast Soviet-Russian territories. Development using this system would require such huge quantities of materials and such an endless amount of time that within a few decades this system would become unfeasible." And further: "We must therefore come up with ways and means, using revolutionary measures and exploiting technology to the full, of building mobile fortress vehicles, similar to naval monitors, that would operate on a broad belt of frontier on land like warships on the sea."

The first lines of thought resulted in the machines depicted in the illustrations. Not until the later course of development did the Soviet commissars raise their requirements and demand heavy armament. They would have preferred 380 or 420 mm guns. Professional considerations, however, showed that such plans were initially not feasible. It is unnecessary to go into details here, but it should be mentioned that my first design had only a main turret on the rear part of the vehicle (see silhouette) with a single gun. Two smaller turrets on the front sides each had a 75 mm gun. Soviet-Russian requirements soon resulted in the picture shown here. In any case the dimensions of the vehicle itself remained the same.

Testing of the early machines with operating weights of 27.5, 33, and 110 tons had shown that even specific ground pressures of 8.5 to 11.4 psi could readily be used. The large heavy vehicle, in particular, so compressed the earth beneath its tracks that the sink depth was scarcely greater than the smaller and lighter machines, with a considerably lower specific ground pressure. The experience gathered from trials with the 110-ton breakthrough tank caused no concerns

if the specific load of tracks on the "1,000 ton" was 11.4 psi, which was equivalent to a total track contact area of 186,000 square inches. The track width on each side was 9.8 ft., and the length of the contact area was 65 ft.; thus, $2 \times 9.8 \times 65 = 1,290$ square ft.

Understandably, there were no drive systems on hand for such a vehicle. The difficulty in obtaining usable engines for heavy tanks had been shown during building of the 110-ton tank. The Soviet Russians hastily sent tenders to leading companies all over the world, but not a single one met the stated requirements in the areas of power, dimensions, and weight. The single exception was an authoritative German company, but after thorough examination of the documents, it turned out that this engine was in the prototype stage, and the factory specified a minimum delivery time of eighteen months. But the engine's dimensions were so compact, and the power-to-weight ratio so good, that this engine was used as an example in the development of the larger types of fortress tank. They also turned to ship design and developed combined engines for the propulsion system. A total of twelve 2,000 hp engines were envisaged, in three groups each of four engines. The cylinder bore was $D = 13.75$ inches, the stroke was 15.75 inches, the speed was 600 rpm, and the number of cylinders per engine was sixteen. In each group one engine drove, via a clutch and shaft. a shaft, and these three shafts via gearing drove the main power plant shaft. The latter, as well as the reduction shafts, were divided into left and right groups (port and starboard), so that in this way six engines of the entire propulsion group powered the left and right tracks.

Two main proposals were worked out for infinitely variable speed control. The first envisaged mechanical transmission in combination with a sort of electric brake regulation. This design, proposed by a French electrical company, was very heavy and complicated but promised good effectiveness over a wide operating range. The second project envisaged hydraulic rpm inverters, which, with a somewhat different grouping of the engines, proved very compact.

Other types of propulsion were examined in detail; for example, powered return rollers, which had a considerable diameter. The engines had to be accommodated in the lower part of the vehicle, which would have threatened them if the floor of the vehicle was damaged; equalizing the loads among the individual engines was not easy to achieve.

A French engineer made an interesting proposal for the propulsion system to use high-pressure steam, in the style of

Velox systems, a design used by Brown Boveri & Co. in Baden, Switzerland. Such systems were in use in France, to my knowledge also in marine vessels. The tank's running gear would then be driven by electric motors, which received their power from turbodynamos of the high-pressure steam system. The required performance could not then be achieved in the space available, however; the electrical equipment was too heavy.

Quite extraordinary demands were placed on the running gear; the tremendous weight of the weaponry required first-rate balancing in the running gear. Because of the excellent experience gained with the hydraulic suspension of the 110-ton breakthrough tank, the same principle was used here. The support rollers, about 78.75 inches in diameter and coupled in groups of three, were suspended by cables, whose ends hung from a system of plunger pistons in oil-filled cylinders. The latter were joined together by a pipe system, so that every additional load on one of the support rollers was distributed among all the other support rollers, and in this way an excellent load distribution was achieved on the entire running gear. The 110-ton tank also proved that this suspension provided good damping of all vibrations that developed while the vehicle was moving, so that the same system could be used with confidence in the largest vehicle.

In conclusion, somewhat more about the cost question of such a mammoth vehicle touched on by *Herr* Burstyn. Certainly the Russians can solve the question of border fortifications in other ways. And probably they will solve other things even more unimaginable and even more grotesque to us Europeans. This is because the Soviet Russians do not have the same concept of cost as we. The country has every natural resource in the world in almost inexhaustible quantities; it is also rich in human resources. Present-day Russia needs nothing else. All the existing huge structures of its heavy industry have been created only at the cost of its human resources, by unheard of human sacrifices. But that is Russian, only Russian. The Soviet Bolsheviks work no differently than Peter the Great did, not crueler and not more humane. A people with the hereditary disease of nihilism in its blood does not ask about the costs of mammoth tanks if it builds them to destroy culture and the world. And the Soviet Union will build them, in whatever form!

It is also an undeniable fact that today's projects, which will become reality tomorrow, are under the pressure of utopian conditions of yesterday, on the basis of experiences with a 110- or 165-ton armored vehicle, which shall also be fast. Cannot an even heavier, larger, more powerful combat vehicle be developed—untied to roads and bridges, flattening hills and valleys defended by field guns, fording rivers, and bypassing forests and fortresses, creating a trail for the following motorized train of an army where otherwise there would be insurmountable obstacles?

Development will, however, always be adapted to the conditions of the region in which it will be used, and what might be appropriate for the vast plains of Russia and Siberia might be utopian and useless in the Alpine regions of Europe. Such considerations must therefore be included in all disciplined undertakings in deciding the size of such machines.

Statements by German prisoners of war also contributed to the confusion, as the following document shows:

M.I. 10/4652, dated 29/1/1945:
Secret Summary of Reports Regarding New German Heavy Tanks

No.	Name	Details	Source
1	Tank destroyer	contract for 132 tons, 7 inches of armor	Secret source via neutral country; mass production at Steyr, Austria
2	*Maus*	77–82 tons (estimated), at least 105 mm gun, with diesel engine suspension, stored at Böblingen with *Tiger*; Inventor, Dr. Porsche	Secret source. Informant claims to have guarded hangar gate
3	*Maus*	176 tons, provisional design by Krupp, Essen (2nd mechanical workshop). Under the direction of Dr. Porsche	Hostile civilian
4	*Maus*	132 tons, 13.75 inches of armor on all sides of turret, hull, and superstructure. One 150 mm and two 105 mm guns in turret. Three 12 mm MGs in turret and one in bow	POW, employed in workshop, 12 years civilian and military, experience as auto mechanic. The POW received his information from the crew. The test tank was housed at Böblingen, near Stuttgart

5	*Maus*	The new tank, superior to the *Tiger* and *Panther*, was formerly produced at the Hautana factory in Böblingen, but production was transferred to Linz after very effective bombing	Information via a neutral source
6	*Mäuschen*	121 tons, 120 mm or larger gun caliber, with BMW aero-engine, manufactured by Alkett	A believable but unreliable POW. He admitted that this information was only hearsay
7	*Mäuschen & Mammut*	Two new, completely assembled heavy tanks with at least a 150 mm gun	A very reliable POW, who quoted this as information from his department head. The POW was employed at MNH Hanover until September 1944
8	—	New *Tiger* with round turret and a 105 mm gun.	POW of unknown reliability
9	Adolf Hitler Tank One	Fixed 88 mm and one 88 mm gun in revolving turret in rear. Several 20 mm and smaller automatic weapons Heavily armored and fast. High diesel consumption: 700–1,000 L per 100 km (2.5–3.5 gal./mile)	POW of unknown reliability
10	Eiserner Ferdinand	At least one 180 mm gun	POW (cunning, no character or moral self-control, "Nazified")
11	Eiserner Ferdinand Or Sturer Gustav	One 220 mm howitzer, two 75 mm guns, six MGs, two flamethrowers	Very heavy POW (anti-Nazi, believes that the information is true)

Glossary

AK	Krupp AG department for artillery design (Kruppaka at Fax)
AKP	Subdepartment tank design, light artillery
C 32	Design year
(D)	Daimler-Benz
DL (H)	Henschel
HL	High-performance engine
HWA	*Heereswaffenamt* (Army Ordnance Office)
In 6	Inspectorate of Transportation
In 5	Inspectorate of Engineer Troops
K	*Kanone* (gun)
(K)	Krupp
KwK	*Kampfwagenkanone* (tank gun)
L/5	Shell length five times the caliber
L/55	Barrel length 55 times the caliber
Lafette	Gun carriage
(P)	Porsche
S.K.	Rapid-loading gun
VK 65 01	Experimental design with planned operational weight and version number
Vo	Initial velocity of a shell after leaving the barrel
Wa Prüf	Army Ordnance Office, *Amtsgruppe* for development and testing

Wa Prüf 1	Ballistics and Munitions Department, with four branches
Wa Prüf 2	Infantry Department, small-caliber weapons to 20 mm
Wa Prüf 4	Artillery Department, weapons larger than 20 mm
Wa Prüf 5	Engineer and Railroad Engineer Department
Wa Prüf 6	Motor Transport and Motorization Department, vehicles, tanks, and motorization
Wa Prüf 7	Signals Department
Wa Prüf 8	Department for optics, measurement, army weather service, fire control, and map printing
Wa Prüf 9	Gas Defense Department, gas defense, smoke, and warfare agents
Wa Prüf 10	Department for small-caliber rockets, up to 120 mm caliber
Wa Prüf 11	Department for special equipment, large rockets
Wa Prüf 12	Department for testing sites and *Wa Prüf* economics
WuG 6	*Amtsgruppe* for weapons procurement and tank equipment department

Endnotes

1. Bundesarchiv-Militärarchiv (BA-MA) Freiburg, Bestand RH 8 I-2836, minutes of January 24, 1942.
2. Willi A. Boelcke, ed., *Deutschlands Rüstung im Zweiten Weltkrieg: Hitlers Konferenzen mit Albert Speer 1942–1945* (Frankfurt: Akademische Verlagsgesellschaft Athenaion, 1969).
3. BA-MA Freiburg, RH 8 I-2959.
4. BA-MA Freiburg, RH 8 I-2836.
5. BA-MA Freiburg, RH 8/2854.
6. Boelcke, *Deutschlands Rüstung im Zweiten Weltkrieg*, p. 205.
7. BA-MA Freiburg, Bestand RH 8/2837.
8. BA R3/1593.
9. BA-MA Freiburg, Bestand RH 8 I/2853.
10. Boelcke, *Deutschlands Rüstung im Zweiten Weltkrieg*, pp. 368–396.
11. BA-MA Freiburg, RH 8 I 2850.
12. BA-MA Freiburg, RH 8 I 2851.
13. BA-MA Freiburg, RH 8 I 2625.
14. Wolfgang Schneider and Frank Köhler, *Tiger im Kampf*, vol. 3 (Uelzen, Germany: Schneider Armour Research, 2013), p. 102.
15. Boelcke, *Deutschlands Rüstung im Zweiten Weltkrieg*, p. 162.
16. BA-MA Freiburg, RH 8/2971.
17. Spec sheets for army weapons, vehicles, and equipment.
18. EH 8/2971.
19. Boelcke, *Deutschlands Rüstung im Zweiten Weltkrieg*, p. 396.
20. Boelcke, *Deutschlands Rüstung im Zweiten Weltkrieg*, p. 411.
21. BA-MA Freiburg, RH 8/2971.
22. "Overview of the State of Developments in the Army," No. 661/42 g.Kdos. *Wa Prüf Stab* of July 1, 1942.
23. BA-MA Freiburg, RH 8-2984.
24. BA-MA Freiburg, RH 8-2983.
25. BA-MA Freiburg, RH 8-2984.
26. BA-MA Freiburg, RH 8-2983, sheet 24.
27. Herbert A. Quint, *Porsche: Der Weg eines Zeitalters* (Stuttgart: Steingrüben-Verlag, 1951), p. 148.
28. Karl-Otto Saur and Michael Saur, *Er stand in Hitlers Testament: Ein deutsches Familienerbe* (Berlin: Ullstein Buchverlage, 2007), p. 204.
29. M. Kolomnez, *Landschiffe Stalins* (Moscow: Russia-Exmo, 2009), p. 174.
30. *Die Kraftfahrkampftruppe* 9 (1939).
31. Boelcke, *Deutschlands Rüstung im Zweiten Weltkrieg*, p. 136.
32. Albert Speer, *Spandauer Tagebücher*, 2d ed. (Berlin: Ullstein, 2011), p. 59.
33. BA-MA Freiburg, RH 8/2976.
34. *Waffen-Revue* 78 (1990).
35. Walter J. Spielberger, *Der Panzer-Kampswagen Tiger und seine Abarten* (Stuttgart, Motorbuch Verlag, 2003), p. 138; tank production in the Second World War.
36. BA-MA Freiburg, RH 8/2986.
37. Ibid.
38. Ibid.
39. Emil Leeb, *Aus der Rüstung des Dritten Reiches (Das Heereswaffenamt 1938–1945)* (Berlin: E. S. Mittler & Sohn Verlag, 1958).
40. Wilhelm Treue and Stefan Zima, *Hochleistungsmotoren–Karl Maybach und sein Werk* (Düsseldorf: VDI Verlag, 1992), p. 46.
41. *Das Personenlexikon zum Dritten Reich*, p. 521.

Bibliography

Boelcke, Willi A., ed. *Deutschlands Rüstung im Zweiten Weltkrieg: Hitlers Konferenzen mit Albert Speer 1942–1945*. Frankfurt: Akademische Verlagsgesellschaft Athenaion, 1969.

Bundesarchiv-Militärarchiv (BA-MA) Freiburg, Bestand RH 8 I Teil 1 bis 3, Akte 1750, 2513, 2625, 2796, 2834, 2835, 2836, 2837, 2850, 2851, 2852, 2854, 2856, 2959, 2976, 2978, 2980, 2983, 2984, 2985, 2986, 2987, 2988, 3030, 3055, 3162, 3165, 3276, 3283, 3514, 3534, 3871, 3926, 3945, 3954, 3971.

D 656/43 Tiger-Ausführung B: Handbuch für den Panzerfahrer. Vol. 1, September 1, 1944.

Datenblätter für Heeres-Waffen, -Fahrzeuge und -Gerät. Nürnberg, Germany: Pawlas, 1976.

Klee, Ernst. *Das Personenlexikon zum Dritten Reich*. Frankfurt: S. Fischer-Verlag, 2003.

Knittel, Hartmut H. *Panzerfertigung im Zweiten Weltkrieg*. Bonn, Germany: Verlag E. S. Mittler & Sohn, 1988.

Köhler, Frank. *Panther-Meilenstein der Panzertechnik*. Uelzen, Germany: Schneider Armour Research, 2014.

Kolomnez, M. *Landschiffe Stalins*. Moscow: Russia-Exmo, 2009.

Leeb, Emil, General der Artillerie. *Aus der Rüstung des Dritten Reiches (Das Heereswaffenamt 1938–1945)*. Berlin: E. S. Mittler & Sohn Verlag, May 1958.

Möller, Eberhard, and Werner Brack. *Einhundert Jahre Dieselmotoren für fünf deutsche Marinen*. Hamburg, Germany: Verlag E. S. Mittler & Sohn, 1998.

Pawlas, Karl R. *Waffenrevue Nr. 44, 78, 84, 91*. Schwäbisch Hall, Germany: Pawlas-Verlag, 1990.

Quint, Herbert A. *Porsche: Ein Weg eines Zeitalters*. Stuttgart: Steingrüben-Verlag, 1951.

Saur, Karl-Otto, and Michael Saur. *Er stand in Hitlers Testament: Ein deutsches Familienerbe*. Berlin: Ullstein Buchverlage, 2007.

Schneider, Wolfgang, and Frank Köhler. *Tiger im Kampf*. Vol. 3. Uelzen, Germany: Schneider Armour Research, 2013.

Schwarzmann, Peter. *Panzerketten: Die Gleisketten der deutschen Kettenfahrzeuge des Zweiten Weltkrieges*. Königswinter, Germany: Brandenburgisches Verlagshaus, 2013.

Spielberger, Walter J. *Spezial-Panzer-Fahrzeuge des deutschen Heeres*, Stuttgart: Motorbuch Verlag, 1977.

——. *Der Panzerkampfwagen Tiger und seine Abarten*. Stuttgart: Motorbuch Verlag, 2003.

——. *Leichte Jagdpanzer: Entwicklung, Fertigung, Einsatz*. Stuttgart: Motorbuch Verlag, 2011.

Taube, Gerhard. *Eisenbahngeschütz DORA: Das größte Geschütz aller Zeiten*. Stuttgart: Motorbuch Verlag, 1979.

——. *Die schwersten Steilfeuer-Geschütze, 1914–1945*. Stuttgart: Motorbuch Verlag, 1981.

Treue, Wilhelm, and Stefan Zima. *Hochleistungsmotoren Karl Maybach und sein Werk*. Düsseldorf: VDI Verlag, 1992.

Photo Credits

W. J. Spielberger Collection (pp. 21, 26, 27, 32, 34–37, 40–43, 47–49, 50, 52–69, 78, 79, 90, 91)

Yuri Pasholok Collection (pp. 104, 106, 109, 112, 113, 115–118, 120, 123–131)

Joachim Deppmeyer Collection (pp. 22, 24)

WTS Koblenz (p. 51)

BA/BA-MA (pp. 70, 74)

National Archives & Records Administration, Washington, DC (pp. 86, 87, 88, 89, 99, 101)

Schneider Armour Research Verlag (p. 44)

Porsche Historisches Archiv (pp. 20, 35, 45, 153, 154, 156, 159)

Tank Museum Bovington Archive (p. 69)

Mercedes-Benz Classic Archive (pp. 114, 122, 149)

Bayerische Staatsbibliothek–Hoffmann Archiv (pp. 131, 138, 144, 145)

Wolfgang Fleischer Collection (pp. 103, 110, 111, 112)

Gunpoint-3D.com (p. 16)

Erik Ritterbach (p. 133)

Falk Springer "*Fahrzeuge der Wehrmacht*" (p. 97)

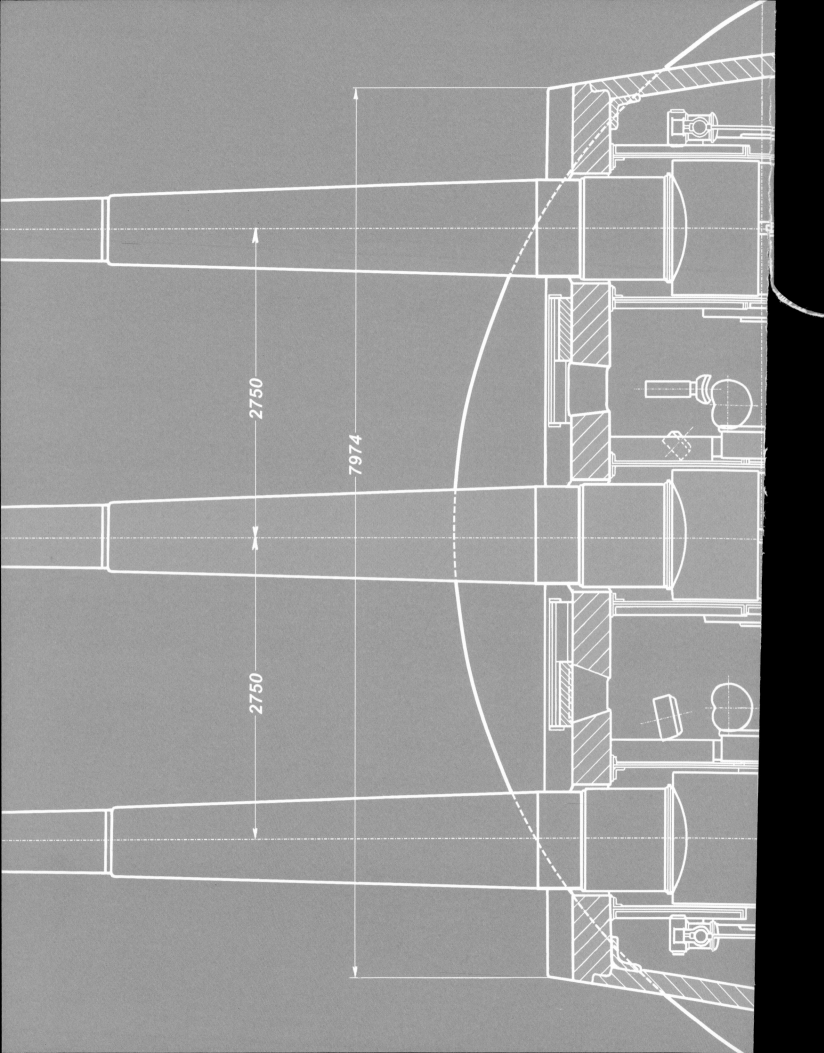